THE OFFICIAL
BRIDGERTON
GUIDE TO ENTERTAINING

HOW TO
COOK, HOST, AND TOAST
LIKE A MEMBER OF THE TON

Emily Timberlake

Photographs by Lizzie Munro
Recipes by Susan Vu

shondaland | NETFLIX

RANDOM HOUSE
WORLDS

Contents

CHAPTER 4

Dinner at the Featherington Ball 93

CHAPTER 5

Lady Danbury's Den of Iniquity 127

Introduction

"*Miss Patridge requires large amounts of sugar for her morning tea, and Lord Abernathy, he will refuse to eat any meat that is not well cooked, while Lady Abernathy will only consume her meat bloody, I am told.*"

—LADY VIOLET BRIDGERTON, TO HER HOUSEKEEPER

For members of the ton, life is an uninterrupted parade of morning visits, al fresco luncheons, dinners, balls, and other social obligations. To most of us, it sounds like a charmed existence: flitting from party to party, with an occasional stop at the modiste to pick up a new dress or Gunter's for tea and ice cream. But ask any ambitious mama, and she will tell you that entertaining (and being entertained) is no trifling matter. Lives, fortunes, and the sanctity of ancient family lineages depend on it.

At its heart, the London social season is an opportunity for the most powerful families of Great Britain to forge alliances. "Most marriages of the ton are, in fact, mere matters of business, my dear," Lady Danbury tells Kate Sharma. But unlike barristers and bankers, members of the English aristocracy do not have offices. Instead, their work takes place on promenades through Hyde Park, over tea in Mayfair drawing rooms, or on hunts at country estates.

All of this means that the stakes for any given party are extremely high. Being a poor hostess is simply not an option. If your lemonade is too sweet (or not sweet enough), your meat pies are too dry, or your dessert table isn't sufficiently overabundant, then people will talk. Worse still, they will leave early and refuse future invitations.

It is no coincidence that the families with the best cooks also have the happiest and most robust social lives. When your intended guest is choosing between two equally compelling breakfast invitations, being able to offer a consistently delicious cup of tea will give you the competitive edge. If you can also promise cream-filled profiteroles (page 121) and crumbly bacon scones (page 137), then their acceptance of your invitation is all but guaranteed.

The book you are holding distills the secrets of the best hosts and hostesses of the ton. Their cooks have graciously shared more than forty recipes for finger foods and libations—everything you could possibly need to host your own *Bridgerton*-inspired soirée. Nobody knows her way around a Blackberry and Citrus Curd Bar (page 143) better than Lady Danbury, and Violet Bridgerton's Miniature Pommes Anna (page 27) are the stuff of legend. Learn how to make a fragrant Masala Chai (page 85) à la Kate Sharma, and you might find a viscount who loves you, too.

In addition to the recipes for beverages and hors d'oeuvres, you will find special features that demystify some of the more arcane rules of English high society. If these rules seem confusing, it is very much by design. It is easy to identify outsiders if they don't know how to curtsy or understand the difference between a countess and a viscountess. But with this book as your guide, you will be able to navigate even the most exclusive social situation with grace.

If this book inspires you to gather your nearest and dearest around you, then it has done its job. It doesn't matter whether you're celebrating a birthday, engagement, the launch of a new social season, or merely the end of a long workweek. Regardless of the occasion, the recipes that follow guarantee a good time will be had by all.

May your parties be delicious, well attended, and fruitful!

1

A Breakfast Visit with the Bridgertons

"Have Cook prepare as many biscuits as he can this morning. . . . I do wonder which gentleman will be the very first to call."

—DAPHNE BRIDGERTON

Lady Violet Bridgerton is an optimist, which is why her breakfast table teems with biscuits, scones, cakes, brioches, fruits, and savories throughout the London season—especially on mornings following a ball. Violet would never be caught empty-handed, or empty-tabled, with a horde of eligible bachelors chomping at her doorstep. If her daughters' suitors are short on appetite, the Bridgerton children can be counted on to make quick work of any excess. When it comes to both affairs of the heart and the morning repast, Lady Bridgerton feels it is best to err on the side of extravagance.

Will the Bridgertons' biscuits help you cement your own love match? It is impossible to say. But even if you are not on the Marriage Mart, a fine breakfast will fortify you for the day ahead. If friends or lovers stop by to share it with you, all the better.

Brunch

Though many Regency breakfasts were simple affairs of toast, butter, and a fine pot of marmalade, some mornings merit a bit more pomp and pageantry. Even if you aren't expecting suitors, a Sunday brunch can be just the thing after a special event: a way to debrief about the night before, or a special event all on its own.

DÉCOR

Instead of a traditional sit-down meal, serve brunch buffet-style to free yourself up to enjoy your guests. Weather permitting, set your table next to a window to take advantage of the warm, midmorning sun. Lay out place mats, napkins, silverware, and glassware, then stack plates next to an appealing spread of food. Add a bright bowl of citrus fruit or berries and a colorful, informal bouquet to contribute to the cheery mood.

FOOD + DRINK

You'll want to feature three or four dishes, some that you can make (or at least prep) the day before, and some that are best served right out of the oven. Make sure to mix and match sweet and savory options, and consider setting out a large bowl of fresh, seasonal fruit. For bigger parties, it's easiest to create serve-yourself coffee and tea stations for guests. In addition to milk, cream, sugar, and sliced lemons, consider offering a special add-in for coffee and tea, such as the Vanilla Bean–Honey Syrup featured in the London Fog Latte recipe (page 33) or the Brown Sugar and Treacle Syrup (page 151). Several carafes of fresh fruit juices are a beautiful and delicious addition to any breakfast table. It is up to you whether you choose to augment them with sparkling wine (see Sparkling Cocktail Bar, page 29).

Throughout history—since well before the Regency era and up to the modern day—the same aggravation has plagued party hosts around the world: *tardiness*. There is nothing worse than watching your carefully crafted meal cool to room temperature as guests wander to the table twenty minutes later than intended. But when it comes to breakfast and brunch, the opposite is often true: Your guests are likely to show up on time, or even ahead of schedule, in desperate need of food and caffeine. Be ready to go at the appointed time and be prepared for the dreaded doorbell ring . . . half an hour early. If the early bird is someone you know well, put them to work! You can reserve an easy job (slicing lemons or chopping chives) to occupy the first to arrive and make them feel helpful. Or you can greet the guests enthusiastically, offer them cups of their preferred brews, and invite them to sit on the couch or in the garden while you finish your preparations.

CRUMPETS
with Salted Honey Butter

Makes 10 to 14 crumpets (depending on size)

SALTED HONEY BUTTER

¾ cup / 165g unsalted butter, at room temperature
3 to 4 tablespoons honey, plus additional for drizzling
1 teaspoon kosher salt, plus additional as needed

CRUMPETS

1 tablespoon unsalted butter
1¾ cups / 475ml water, plus additional for thinning the batter
½ cup / 120ml whole milk
2 teaspoons honey
One ¼-ounce / 7g packet active dry yeast
1¼ cups / 175g all-purpose flour
¾ cup / 105g bread flour
2 teaspoons baking powder
1¼ teaspoons kosher salt
Vegetable oil for greasing the skillet and molds
Fruit preserves and/or marmalade to serve

Special Equipment: Four crumpet or English muffin molds (about 3½ inches / 8.9cm in diameter; see Cook's Note)

A crumpet is a small, round bread cooked on a griddle—similar to what Americans call "English muffins." Violet Bridgerton has yet to encounter a crumpet better than her cook's: They are soft and spongy, with just the right number of craggy pockets to catch butter and jam.

Cook's Note: If you do not have crumpet or English muffin molds, you can also use large Mason jar lids or clean tuna fish cans to create the round shape.

FOR THE HONEY BUTTER: In a small bowl, combine the butter, 3 tablespoons of the honey, and salt. Stir until smooth. Taste the flavored butter and adjust with more honey or salt depending on your preference. Set aside at room temperature.

FOR THE CRUMPETS: In a small saucepan over medium heat, melt the butter until it starts to bubble, about 2 minutes. Remove from the heat and stir in 1½ cups / 360ml of the water and the milk. The residual heat in the saucepan should make this mixture lukewarm. If the mixture becomes hot, let it cool until it's lukewarm. Set it aside while you prepare the yeast.

In a small bowl, stir together the remaining ¼ cup / 60ml of water and the 2 teaspoons of honey. Sprinkle the yeast on top, stir to combine slightly, then set aside until foamy, about 2 minutes.

In a large bowl combine the all-purpose flour and bread flour. Add the yeast mixture and the lukewarm milk mixture. Whisk vigorously for 3 minutes and set aside.

Cover the bowl and set aside until the mixture is slightly risen and lightly foamy and bubbly on top, about 45 minutes. Whisk the batter a couple of times; it should have the consistency of crepe batter (a fair amount thinner than pancake batter) and pour easily off a spoon. Whisk in the baking powder and 1¼ teaspoons salt. Set aside until it is foamy and bubbly again, about 20 additional minutes.

Recipe continues

☛ Heat a large, well-seasoned cast-iron skillet between medium and medium-high heat. Dip a rolled-up paper towel in a bit of vegetable oil and use tongs to grease the skillet with the oil. The skillet should be lightly coated with oil. Dip a second paper towel in oil and grease the inside of four crumpet or English muffin molds and place them in the skillet. Give the batter a good whisk, which will help to get it nice and bubbly, then fill each ring with ¼ to ⅓ cup / 55 to 75g of the batter (depending on how thick you want your crumpets to be).

☛ Cook for exactly 3 minutes, then lower the heat to medium and continue to cook until the tops of the crumpets are filled with bubbles that have popped, the edges and tops of the batter are set, and the bottoms are golden brown, 7 to 10 minutes. Adjust the heat as needed if the bottoms are getting too brown before the tops are set; rotate the skillet several times during the cooking process to ensure even browning. Use tongs to carefully remove the molds, flip the crumpets, and increase the heat again to between medium and medium-high heat. Cook on the second side until the crumpets are completely cooked through and the second side is lightly golden brown, 3 to 6 additional minutes. Flip the crumpets over again so that they are hole-side up, then transfer to a wire rack.

☛ Repeat the cooking method with the remaining batter, whisking 1 to 2 teaspoons of additional water into the batter after each batch. This will help to keep the batter thin and also ensure active bubbling even as the batter sits. Grease the skillet and molds again after each batch.

☛ Once the last crumpets come out of the skillet, allow them to cool for a full 10 minutes before serving the crumpets warm or cool completely, then toast in a 350°F / 175°C oven for 7 to 10 minutes, until they become warm and toasty. Serve warm with the salted honey butter and your favorite fruit preserves and/or marmalade, or drizzle with honey.

MEYER LEMON AND POPPY SEED TEA BISCUITS

"THE FASTEST COURTSHIP UPON RECORD OCCURRED DURING THE MARKEDLY WET SEASON OF 1804, WHEN MISS MARY LEOPOLD SECURED A BETROTHAL OVER A PLATE OF SUGARED ALMONDS AND LICORICE IN JUST FOUR AND A HALF MINUTES."
—LADY WHISTLEDOWN

Makes 32 biscuits

⅓ cup / 80ml plus
   1 tablespoon milk
2 tablespoons fresh Meyer
   lemon juice
1 cup / 140g all-purpose flour,
   plus additional for dusting
1 cup / 140g whole wheat flour
1¼ teaspoons baking powder
1 tablespoon poppy seeds
½ teaspoon kosher salt
½ cup / 110g (1 stick) unsalted
   butter, at room temperature
1 cup / 120g confectioners'
   sugar
1 tablespoon finely grated fresh
   Meyer lemon zest

Special Equipment: One
   3-inch / 7.5cm heart-shaped
   cookie cutter

If the Marriage Mart were to have an official headquarters, it would most certainly be Gunter's Tea Shop. Gunter's is the site of many of the ton's most famous (and famously speedy) courtships. Evidently, a generously sugared confection is just the thing to put eligible men and women into a matrimonial mood. If you cannot make it to Berkeley Square, try baking these delightful treats in your own home. They are marvelous alongside a cup of Earl Grey tea, and a worthy alternative to anything you'd find in Gunter's shop window.

☞ In a small bowl, stir together the milk and lemon juice. Set aside for 10 minutes. The milk will curdle during this time and will mimic the consistency of buttermilk. In a medium bowl, whisk together the all-purpose flour, whole wheat flour, baking powder, poppy seeds, and salt. Set aside.

☞ In a large bowl, combine the butter, confectioners' sugar, and lemon zest. Use an electric hand mixer on low speed to blend until the mixture is smooth. Add the flour mixture and blend on low speed until combined, with the butter broken into very small pieces and the mixture almost pebbly in texture. Drizzle the milk mixture over and blend on low speed until a crumbly dough forms. Do not overmix; some dry patches of flour are okay. Use your hands to pat the dough together, kneading it a couple of times directly in the bowl, until it is smooth. Divide the dough in two, then place each mound of dough onto its own piece of plastic wrap. Pat each into a 1-inch / 2.5cm thick disk and chill in the refrigerator for 30 minutes. The dough will firm up slightly during this time and be easier to roll out.

Recipe continues

☞ Preheat the oven to 350°F / 175°C. Line two baking sheets with parchment paper and set aside.

☞ Generously dust a work surface with flour, then roll one of the chilled dough disks out until it is just a touch thicker than ⅛ inch / 3mm thick. Lightly flour a 3-inch / 7.5cm heart-shaped cookie cutter and cut the dough into sixteen biscuits, rerolling the scraps as needed. As you are rolling and cutting, dust the dough and work surface with more flour as needed to prevent sticking. Dust any excess flour off the biscuits with a dry pastry brush.

☞ Place the biscuits on one of the prepared baking sheets. They will not spread so it is okay to arrange them closely, but the biscuits should not be touching. Prick each biscuit several times with a fork and bake until the edges and bottoms are light golden brown and the tops are firm, 20 to 25 minutes, rotating the baking sheet once after 10 minutes.

☞ While the first batch of biscuits is baking, roll and cut out the second dough disk and place the biscuits on the second prepared baking sheet.

☞ Remove the baked biscuits from the oven and cool completely on the hot baking sheet. The biscuits will crisp up as they cool. Repeat the baking and cooling process with the second batch of biscuits. Serve with your favorite hot tea. Store any leftover biscuits in an airtight container at room temperature for up to 7 days.

CRUSTLESS QUICHE
with Caramelized Leek, Ham, and English Cheddar

Makes 8 to 12 servings

1½ tablespoons unsalted butter, plus additional for greasing

1 large leek

Kosher salt and freshly ground black pepper

8 ounces / 225g ham, preferably Wiltshire cured ham, finely diced (about 1½ cups), patted dry

4 ounces / 115g aged English cheddar cheese, shredded (about 1¼ cups)

8 large eggs

⅔ cup / 160ml heavy cream

3 tablespoons coarsely chopped fresh flat-leaf parsley

Pinch of cayenne pepper

This quiche is a celebration of several of England's finest culinary products: pungent leeks, which populate the countryside from autumn through late winter; succulent Wiltshire ham; and sharp cheddar. The ingredients are mixed with farm-fresh eggs and baked in a pie pan, resulting in the most aromatic breakfast pie imaginable.

Cook's Notes: Any cooked meat can be used here in place of the ham: Try crumbled breakfast sausage, shredded chicken, or chopped leftover pot roast. Alternatively, make it vegetarian by using sautéed wild mushrooms or additional roasted vegetables.

If you'd prefer to make petite individual quiches instead of one larger quiche, pour the egg mixture into the cups of standard nonstick muffin pans and bake until just set and golden brown in spots, about 25 minutes.

☞ Place a baking sheet on the center rack of the oven and preheat to 350°F / 175°C. Grease a 9½-inch / 24.1cm deep dish pie plate with butter and set aside.

☞ Cut away the tough dark green top and root end from the leek, then quarter the remainder of the leek lengthwise. Thinly slice each leek quarter crosswise into ⅛-inch / 3mm thick pieces (about 2 cups / 170g). Transfer the sliced leek into a medium bowl, fill the bowl with cold water, and use your hands to separate the leek pieces and coax out any dirt. Drain through a fine-mesh strainer and repeat this process until there is no dirt left on the leek pieces. Dry the leek pieces well.

☞ In a medium skillet over medium heat, melt half of the butter. Add the leek pieces, season with salt and pepper, and cook, stirring occasionally, until the leek is very tender, about 15 minutes. Transfer the cooked leek pieces to a medium bowl, then increase the heat slightly and add the remaining butter. Once the butter is melted, add the ham and cook, stirring occasionally, until lightly browned in spots, about 5 minutes. Some

Recipe continues

types of ham might exude a lot of water and not brown and that is okay. Tilt the skillet and remove any excess liquid that pools at the bottom and continue cooking until the ham is lightly browned. Transfer to the same bowl as the cooked leek and set aside.

☞ Scatter half of the English cheddar cheese on the bottom of the prepared pie plate, then top with the leek and ham mixture. In a large bowl, combine the eggs, heavy cream, parsley, cayenne, and ¾ teaspoon salt and whisk until well combined. Pour into the pie plate, then sprinkle the remaining cheddar cheese on top. Bake on the hot baking sheet until the quiche is set (a cake tester or wooden skewer inserted into the center should come out clean) and lightly golden brown in spots, 40 to 50 minutes, rotating the baking sheet once after 20 minutes. Transfer the pie plate to a wire rack and use a small offset spatula or butter knife to release the sides of the quiche from the pie plate. Cool for at least 30 minutes and up to 2 hours (the longer it sits, the easier it will be to cut into thin serving pieces, if desired). Use a serrated knife to slice the warm quiche into 8 to 12 wedges and serve.

KIPPERS ON TOAST

"KIPPERS ON RYE EVERY MORNING WORKED WONDERS FOR ME
WHEN I CONCEIVED MY NIGEL." —LADY BERBROOKE

Makes 16 pieces

2 large shallots, sliced into
⅟₁₆-inch / 2mm rounds
(about 1 cup / 110g)

2 tablespoons granulated sugar

1½ teaspoons kosher salt, plus
additional if needed

1 teaspoon yellow mustard
seeds

½ cup / 120ml red wine vinegar

⅓ cup / 80ml water

⅓ cup / 80g good-quality
mayonnaise

2 teaspoons prepared English
mustard, such as Colman's

¼ cup / 30g finely chopped
celery

1 tablespoon capers, drained
and coarsely chopped

2 tablespoons coarsely chopped
fresh dill, plus additional
hand-torn dill for garnish

2 tablespoons thinly sliced
green onions

Freshly ground black pepper

Three 3.25 to 3.75-ounce /
90 to 105g cans boneless,
skinless kipper snacks,
drained and flaked

3 tablespoons unsalted butter,
melted

8 thin slices white sandwich
bread, crusts removed and
halved diagonally

Kippers are a favorite among ambitious mamas of the ton who aspire to become grandmamas. Whether or not you believe in the fertility benefits of consuming the fish is up to you, though this author has heard of no immaculate, kipper-induced conceptions. Violet Bridgerton keeps this creamy, tangy whitefish salad on her breakfast table for the simple reason that it is delicious, especially when served on freshly griddled toast.

Cook's Note: Kipper snacks are another name for salted and smoked herring. They can be found in the canned fish section of many supermarkets. If you cannot find kippers, substitute smoked albacore tuna, smoked trout, or hot-smoked salmon.

☞ Put the sliced shallots in a small heatproof glass bowl.

☞ In a small saucepan, stir together the sugar, salt, mustard seeds, red wine vinegar, and water. Bring to a boil over medium heat and cook, stirring occasionally, until the sugar and salt completely dissolve, about 5 minutes.

☞ Pour the hot vinegar mixture over the shallots and stir to combine. Cool the pickled shallots completely at room temperature, about 1 hour.

☞ To make the whitefish salad, in a medium bowl, stir together the mayonnaise, mustard, 1 tablespoon of the pickled shallot brine, the celery, capers, dill, green onions, and several grinds of black pepper. Fold in the flaked kipper snacks. Taste and season with salt. Cover and refrigerate while you toast the bread.

☞ Preheat the oven to 325°F / 165°C.

☞ Heat a large cast-iron skillet over medium heat. Brush both sides of the bread with the melted butter. In batches, toast the buttered bread in the hot skillet until lightly browned, about 2 minutes per side. Transfer to a baking sheet, then bake in the oven until the bread is crispy throughout, about 10 minutes. Allow to cool for 5 minutes.

☞ To serve, spread the whitefish salad onto the toasted bread and top with the drained pickled shallots. Garnish with the dill.

MINIATURE POMMES ANNA

Makes 12 servings

6 tablespoons / 85g unsalted butter, plus additional for greasing
1 teaspoon chopped fresh rosemary leaves
2 garlic cloves, finely grated
1½ pounds / 680g baby Dutch yellow potatoes (12 to 16 total, each no wider than 1½ inches / 4cm)
Kosher salt and freshly ground black pepper
2 ounces / 55g Gruyère cheese, finely grated (about 2 cups)
1 tablespoon thinly sliced chives

Pommes Anna is a classic French dish of thinly sliced potatoes, which are shingled in multiple layers to build a rosette-shaped potato cake. The end result is breathtaking, but the cooking technique is notoriously difficult. This miniaturized version is as delicious as the original but less vexing. To make this truly extraordinary, try adding a dollop of crème fraîche and a spoonful of caviar on top of each pomme Anna. The Frenchman who invented the dish would applaud you.

☞ Preheat the oven to 350°F / 175°C. Generously butter a 12-cup muffin pan and set aside.

☞ In a small saucepan over medium heat, combine the butter, chopped rosemary, and grated garlic. Cook, stirring occasionally, until the butter is melted and just starting to bubble around the edges of the saucepan, about 3 minutes. Remove from the heat and set aside.

☞ Using a mandoline, slice each potato crosswise into very thin rounds (about ¹⁄₁₆ inch / 2mm thick). Transfer into a large bowl, season with salt and pepper, then drizzle with the butter mixture. Toss well to coat.

☞ Place one potato slice in the center of each muffin cup. Arrange a slightly overlapping layer of additional potato slices on top of the single potato slice, working in a circular pattern. This layer will become the top of the pommes Anna, so take your time to make sure that it looks nice and neat. Scatter a quarter of the grated Gruyère on top of the potatoes, then top with another layer of potato slices and another quarter of the cheese. Repeat this layering process two additional times. After the last layer of cheese, top each cup with a final layer of potato slices using up whatever slices are still left.

☞ When the muffin cups are filled, use the back of a small measuring cup to press down on the potato stacks so that they

Recipe continues

are flat on top and compact. Cover the muffin pan tightly with aluminum foil and place the muffin pan on a baking sheet.

☞ Bake for 20 minutes. Remove the foil (reserve to use later in this recipe) and cook, uncovered, until the potatoes are fork-tender and the tops are starting to brown around the edges, about 25 additional minutes. Place the muffin pan on a wire rack to cool for 15 minutes. Use a small offset spatula to immediately loosen the sides of each cup.

☞ Increase the oven temperature to 450°F / 230°C.

☞ Let the baking sheet cool, then line with the reserved foil. Use a small offset spatula to loosen the sides of each cup again, then invert the muffin pan onto the foil-lined baking sheet, banging the pan down on the baking sheet several times to loosen the potatoes.

☞ Bake for 10 minutes, or until the bottoms of the potato stacks are golden brown in spots. Remove from the oven and use two small flat spatulas to carefully flip each potato stack over. Return to the oven and bake until the potato stacks are golden brown and crispy all over, about 10 additional minutes, paying close attention to the bottom of the stacks (those will become the top of the pommes Anna for serving).

☞ Cool on the hot baking sheet for 5 minutes. Flip over each pommes Anna so that the bottom is now the top, garnish with sliced chives, transfer to a platter, and serve.

SPARKLING COCKTAIL BAR

"I DID NOT OVERINDULGE.
TRULY, IT WAS JUST A POOR NIGHT OF SLEEP."
—VIOLET BRIDGERTON

Makes 1 serving

1½ to 2 ounces / 44 to 60ml
   fresh fruit puree or juice (see
   Cook's Notes), or to taste
Sparkling wine (see Cook's
   Notes), chilled, to top
Fresh fruit, for garnish

On the morning after a particularly raucous ball, you might find you require a bit of venom from the snake that bit you. In those situations, no sight is more welcome than a carafe of sparkling wine cocktails perched upon the breakfast table. Use the following recipe as a template: Experiment with whichever seasonal fruit juices or purees strike your fancy (and seem most restorative). Consider offering several different fruit juices or purees, each labeled and in a small carafe, with bowls of freshly cut fruit for garnish. Encourage your guests to mix their own drinks—as many as they require.

Cook's Notes: Freshly squeezed orange juice is the traditional choice for a mimosa-style cocktail; however, grapefruit juice, pomegranate juice, pineapple juice, and fresh apple cider all work well. White peach puree is the standard for a Bellini, but try fresh or frozen (then thawed) puree of passion fruit, mango, or raspberry.

For the wine, pick something high-quality that you would happily drink on its own. The Bridgertons would, of course, fetch one of their finest bottles of Champagne. We commoners can simply ask our local wine merchant to recommend a pleasant Crémant, Cava, or prosecco.

☛ Pour the fruit puree or juice into a flute or coupe. Top with the sparkling wine, garnish with the fresh fruit, and serve.

The Art of the Calling Card

Since the most illustrious families of the ton all live in the same one-square-mile patch of Mayfair, you might assume that paying social calls is as simple as knocking on your neighbors' doors to see if they are at home. But we are discussing the highest echelons of English society—so, of course, nothing is simple.

In London, it is considered acceptable for a lady to visit someone who is her social equal or inferior, but not her social superior. (The rules are slightly more relaxed in the country, which is why many people prefer their estates to the stiff formality of city living.) Practically every door is open to the Duchess of Hastings, who may call upon whomever she pleases whenever she pleases. But a baroness or mere lady has fewer options. If she would like to make the acquaintance of a countess or viscountess, she must wait for the latter to call upon her first.

One can hardly be expected to sit at home waiting all day on the off chance some rich and powerful patroness will call.

This is where the calling card comes into play—an elegant custom that enables ladies to leave their homes without fear of missing a life-changing visit.

On its surface, a calling card is quite simple: It is a small piece of card stock with one's name, title, and perhaps one's address inscribed upon it. If you'd like to initiate contact with a stranger, or if you call on someone who is unavailable for any reason, you simply leave your calling card with a servant. Once a high-ranking lady has left her calling card with someone of a lower station, then that second lady is finally free to call upon her superior.

The calling card is more than just a slender slip of paper. It is also a rare opportunity for a well-bred lady or gentleman to indulge their artistic sensibilities. The ton might whisper—or, worse, Lady Whistledown might take you down with a flick of her quill—if you debut unusual attire or an avant-garde hairstyle. But no one will look askance at a calling card with a bit of panache. And so, asking a line engraver to develop a custom script, design, or original

artwork for you is a safe, socially acceptable way to flaunt your personal style.

Calling cards may seem like a needless relic in our modern, digital age. But there is something to be said for creating a signature that is uniquely your own. The next time you send an invitation—it could be via email, text message, or better yet by post—consider embedding an image of your own customized calling card. Find a font that suits you, embellish it with an attractive border, and consider adding line art that speaks to your name or profession. This is your own personalized coat of arms, and upon receiving it, your friends and family should smile and remark that it is so *you*.

LONDON FOG LATTES

Makes 1 serving

1 cup / 240ml water
2 Earl Grey tea bags
¾ cup / 175ml low-fat or
   whole milk
2 to 3 tablespoons Vanilla
   Bean–Honey Syrup
   (recipe below)

When the clouds hang low and London skies are a too-familiar shade of dreary gray, it is hard to muster the motivation to leave one's bed. This is especially true if one has been dancing and imbibing mulled wine (page 103) the evening prior. But this warm, fragrant drink, with its subtle perfume of whole vanilla bean, is enough to coax even the drowsiest Bridgerton sibling out of bed and into the breakfast room.

☞ In a small teakettle or saucepan over medium heat, bring the water to a boil. Remove from the heat and pour the boiling water into a large mug. Add the Earl Grey tea bags and steep for 5 minutes.

☞ While the tea steeps, in a small saucepan over medium heat, warm the milk until it is hot and steamy, about 3 minutes.

☞ Once the tea has steeped for 5 minutes, remove the tea bags and discard.

☞ When the milk is hot, tip the milk to one side of the saucepan and froth it using a milk frother or by whisking it vigorously until it has doubled in size.

☞ Stir the vanilla-honey syrup into the hot tea, then pour the frothed milk into the tea and spoon any remaining milk froth on top. Serve immediately.

VANILLA BEAN–HONEY SYRUP
Makes 1⅛ cups / 330g

⅓ cup / 65g sugar
⅓ cup / 115g honey
⅔ cup / 160ml water
½ vanilla bean, split and the seeds scraped

☞ In a small saucepan over medium heat, combine the sugar, honey, and water. Bring to a simmer, 5 to 7 minutes, stirring frequently to help the sugar and honey melt evenly. Remove from the heat and add the vanilla bean and seeds. Stir to combine, then let cool to room temperature. Transfer the syrup into a glass jar. Use immediately or store in the refrigerator for up to 1 month.

2

The Queen's Lawn Party

Queen Charlotte must admit that there are some things the French do better than the English. Opulent, indulgent meals happen to be one of them. Take, for example, their *pique-nique*: an al fresco luncheon in which one picks (*piquer*) at small tidbits (*niques*) like savory pies, salads, cakes, and fruits.

A picnic is simple in theory. But in practice, luncheon en plein air requires time, money, and many, many servants. First, you must have access to a stunning location: rolling parkland with sweeping vistas, a well-manicured lawn surrounded by elegant gardens, or a grassy knoll overlooking a picturesque pond.

Then you must have the means to reach said bucolic location: wagons for all the food, plates, cutlery, and linens; carriages for the guests; and servants willing to carry everything to its final destination. (The best and most pastoral sites tend only to be accessible by foot.) This doesn't even touch on the resources required to prepare the actual food, which, if it is to be worthy of a queen, must be flawless.

None of this is meant to dissuade you from throwing your own *petit pique-nique*. Prepare one or several of the recipes that follow, then tuck them into a wicker basket. Spread a blanket on an obliging patch of grass in a local park or your backyard; gaze at the clouds and listen to the breeze. These are the simple pleasures that money, fame, and nobility cannot buy.

37

HOST YOUR OWN

Picnic

You don't need to wait for a special occasion to plan a picnic: Any warm, uncommonly sunny day is cause for celebration. Whether it's a larger event or a romantic moment for two, a little advance planning is all you need to create the perfect idyll.

DÉCOR

If you have access to a picnic table, deck it out with a colorful tablecloth. Weight it down with a bouquet of sunflowers or peonies and your beverages. Pile up plates, cutlery, and napkins at one end and lay out your main course alongside small bowls of treats and snacks. For a more intimate picnic, you'll want a basket or hamper to carry the food in style and a blanket to spread out. If you aren't hiking far, you can bring cozy pillows for sitting and lolling about. Compostable plates and cups are a fine choice, but consider bringing real plates and glassware (stackable Duralex tumblers are a light and sturdy option)—especially if you have a picnic basket with slots to stow them safely.

FOOD + DRINK

Finger foods are perfect for mess-free picnics, whether it's a crusty handheld pie (page 43) or skewered meat (page 51). Supplement these prepared dishes with sliced baguettes or country bread, soft and firm cheeses, cured meat, and berries. Bring a cool and crisp wine for sipping under a shady tree on a hot day, plus a thermos of Lavender Lemonade (page 57) to slake your thirst. When eating outdoors, it is important to leave no trace—so always bring a bag to take away any trash or detritus.

Though good food, good drinks, and plenty of sunshine are the only real requirements, a picnic is made even better by a few optional activities. If you don't have an antique, Regency-era pall-mall set, bring a contemporary croquet or cornhole setup, or keep things simple with a Frisbee. If children (or the young at heart) are in attendance, bring a bubble-blowing set, kite, or guitar. If it's just two of you, bring a deck of cards or a romantic book to read aloud. Or simply lie down on the blanket, gaze up at the sky, and think of nothing at all.

THE DUKE'S GOOSEBERRY HAND PIES

Makes 12 servings

PIE DOUGH

2¼ cups / 315g all-purpose flour, plus more for dusting

1 teaspoon kosher salt

1 cup / 220g (2 sticks) cold unsalted butter, cut into small cubes

2 egg yolks

3 tablespoons ice water, plus additional if needed

3 tablespoons heavy cream

2 tablespoons turbinado sugar (optional)

GOOSEBERRY FILLING

¼ cup / 60ml fresh orange juice

3 tablespoons cornstarch

1-inch / 2.5cm piece fresh ginger, peeled

2 cups / 334g fresh gooseberries or cape gooseberries (see Cook's Note)

1⅔ cups / 330g granulated sugar

Four 2-inch / 5cm strips fresh orange peel

Lady Violet Bridgerton's cook may be renowned for his gooseberry pie, but the queen of England is not one to be outdone by a mere viscountess. So Queen Charlotte set out to develop a gooseberry pie to rival the Bridgertons'; her competitive spirit and affection for the Duke of Hastings demanded it.

Cook's Note: The gooseberry is a large, tart berry native to Northern Europe. It comes in many varieties including green, white, yellow, and red; any variety will work for this recipe. The season runs March through June. If you are unable to find fresh gooseberries, substitute fresh cape gooseberries (also known as goldenberries), which are related to the tomatillo. Make sure to rinse cape gooseberries thoroughly; their exteriors are sticky, like a tomatillo. They tend to have thicker skins so they will take longer to cook.

☞ **FOR THE PIE DOUGH:** In a food processor, combine the flour and salt and pulse to blend. Add the butter and pulse until the mixture resembles coarse meal. Add the egg yolks and pulse one or two more times until they are just incorporated and the dough turns pale yellow. Drizzle in the ice water and pulse until the mixture comes together to form a dough; it does not need to form into a ball, but it should hold together when pinched. If it doesn't, add a small splash of water and pulse again. Transfer the dough to a large piece of plastic wrap and pat the dough into a 1-inch / 2.5cm thick disk. Wrap the dough tightly, then chill in the refrigerator until firm, at least 30 minutes or up to overnight.

☞ **FOR THE FILLING:** In a small bowl, whisk together the orange juice and cornstarch until the cornstarch completely dissolves.

☞ Slice the ginger crosswise into four even pieces, then lightly crush each piece with the flat side of a knife. In a large saucepan or small Dutch oven, combine the ginger, orange juice and cornstarch mixture, gooseberries, sugar, and orange peel and stir to combine. Bring to a boil over medium heat. Continue to boil, stirring occasionally, until the gooseberries burst and the sauce is reduced and thick enough to leave a trail when

Recipe continues

you run a rubber spatula or wooden spoon through it, 10 to 15 minutes. The timing of this will vary depending on the ripeness of the gooseberries. Pour the hot filling into a medium bowl and set aside to cool completely at room temperature. Remove the ginger and orange peel, then cover the bowl and chill in the refrigerator for at least 1 hour and up to 3 days. The filling will continue to thicken as it cools and should ultimately have a slightly firmer consistency than jam.

☛ To assemble and bake: Position two racks in the upper and lower center of the oven and preheat to 375°F / 190°C. Line two baking sheets with parchment paper and set aside.

☛ If you chilled the dough for 30 minutes, it should be ready to roll. If it was in the refrigerator for longer and it is really hard, let it sit at room temperature until it is still firm but manageable to roll. Lightly dust a clean work surface and rolling pin with flour and roll the dough into an ¹⁄₁₆-inch / 2mm thick round, turning the dough every time you roll it to ensure it does not stick. Cut the dough into twelve 5½-inch / 14.3cm rounds; an overturned cereal or soup bowl is usually approximately this size if you do not have a large round cutter. Take any scraps of dough and form them back into a ball, reroll the dough to the same thickness, and continue to cut out all twelve rounds.

☛ Lay one round of dough on the lightly floured work surface and add 2 tablespoons of the cooled filling to the center. Brush the edge of the dough with heavy cream. Fold the top half of the dough over the filling, meeting the bottom edge to form a half-moon shape. Pinch the edges together to seal the dough and remove any excess air. Starting at one edge, fold the dough down along the edge every ⅛ inch / 3mm or so to create a pleated design. Alternatively, you can use a fork to fully seal the edges. Place the hand pie on the prepared baking sheet and repeat with the remaining rounds. Brush the tops of the hand pies with additional heavy cream. Use a paring knife to cut one very small slit into the top. Sprinkle with turbinado sugar (if using).

☛ Place the two baking sheets in the oven and bake until the pies are golden brown all over and the filling just begins to bubble around the vent, about 30 minutes, rotating the baking sheets top to bottom and front to back once after 15 minutes. Remove from the oven and let the pies cool on the baking sheets for 10 minutes. Transfer the hand pies to a platter and serve warm.

LADY DANBURY:
The duke is quite fond of gooseberry pie.

VIOLET BRIDGERTON:
The very dish my cook is renowned for.

CHICKEN LOLLIPOPS
with Red Wine Barbecue Sauce

Makes 24 pieces

12 whole chicken wings (about 3 pounds / 1.4kg)

Kosher salt

One 6-ounce / 170g can tomato paste

1 cup / 240ml full-bodied and fruity red wine, such as Merlot or Pinot Noir

⅓ cup / 80ml red wine vinegar, plus additional to taste

2 tablespoons black treacle (see Cook's Note, page 151)

½ cup / 100g packed light brown sugar

1 tablespoon prepared English mustard, such as Colman's

1½ teaspoons smoked paprika

1½ teaspoons garlic powder

1½ teaspoons onion powder

¼ to ½ teaspoon crushed red pepper flakes

⅛ teaspoon ground allspice

1 tablespoon vegetable oil for greasing baking sheet

2 teaspoons baking powder

The chickens who reside in the royal aviary lead more pampered lives than many of the queen's human subjects. That is, until she decides to host one of her legendary luncheons, at which point several hens must meet their maker. The best way to honor the royal chickens is to ensure that nothing goes to waste. So for this dish, wings are converted to handheld "lollipops" and bathed in a tangy, sweet red wine sauce.

☞ Working with one chicken wing at a time, use a large sharp kitchen knife to cut each chicken wing into three parts, slicing in between the joints. From each chicken wing, you will have a drumette (the piece that resembles a miniature drumstick), a flat (or sometimes called a wingette), and a wing tip. Once all of the chicken wings have been cut, discard the wing tips or save to use for homemade chicken stock.

☞ For the drumettes, switch to a sharp paring knife and very carefully cut around the thin, bony end of the drumette until the skin and meat have released from the bone. Use your hands to push the meat and skin downward toward the meaty end and form the shape of a lollipop. Use a paper towel to help you remove any meat and skin at the top of the bone and use kitchen shears to cut away any tendon. Place the chicken lollipop onto a small baking sheet and repeat with the remaining drumettes.

☞ For the flats, use the paring knife to cut the joint where the two bones meet. Trim some of the meat from around the two bones so that you can remove the smaller bone from the flat. Use your hands to push the meat and skin downward to form the shape of a lollipop. These lollipops will be a little smaller and a little messier than the drumettes, but don't be deterred; just use your hands to mold the meat and skin the best you can. The flats will hold their shape during baking. Clean the top of the bone like you did with the drumettes. Transfer the flats to the same baking sheet as the trimmed drumettes and repeat with the remaining flats. Once all of the chicken lollipops have been

Recipe continues

formed, season the chicken liberally with salt. Chill, uncovered, in the refrigerator while you make the barbecue sauce.

☞ For the barbecue sauce, in a large saucepan over medium heat, combine the tomato paste, red wine, red wine vinegar, treacle, brown sugar, English mustard, smoked paprika, garlic powder, onion powder, red pepper flakes, allspice, and a large pinch of salt; whisk together. Gently warm until the mixture starts to bubble, about 10 minutes, stirring occasionally. Reduce the heat to low and cook at a bare simmer (gentle bubbling), partially covered, stirring occasionally, until the sauce is thickened and the flavors have deepened, about 45 minutes. You should be able to taste the wine, but the sauce should not taste raw and boozy. Season with salt and additional vinegar, if needed. Set aside to cool while you cook the chicken. The sauce will thicken more as it cools.

☞ Preheat the oven to 450°F / 230°C. Line a large rimmed baking sheet with aluminum foil and brush the foil with the vegetable oil.

☞ Pat the chicken dry with paper towels and transfer to a large bowl. Sprinkle with the baking powder and toss to evenly coat. Use your hands to pick up the chicken lollipops, one by one, adjusting the meat and skin if it has shifted, and place on the prepared baking sheet. Bake until lightly browned, crispy, and cooked through, 25 to 30 minutes, rotating the baking sheet once after 15 minutes.

☞ Remove the lollipops from the oven, flip the chicken pieces over, and brush the meat with some of the barbecue sauce. Flip over again, brush with more sauce, then return to the oven. Bake until the sauce is bubbling and browned in spots, about 5 additional minutes. Watch the chicken carefully so that the sauce doesn't burn. Transfer the chicken lollipops to a platter and serve with the remaining barbecue sauce.

SEARED SCALLOPS
with Minted Peas and Browned Butter Walnut Sauce

*Makes
12 servings*

12 large sea scallops (about
1 pound / 450g)
5 tablespoons / 75g unsalted
butter
8 ounces / 225g frozen petite
green peas (about 1⅔ cups),
thawed
¼ cup / 60ml water, plus
additional as needed
Kosher salt and freshly ground
black pepper
⅓ cup / 35g raw walnuts,
coarsely chopped
1 teaspoon finely grated lemon
zest
1 to 2 tablespoons
vegetable oil
12 large fresh mint leaves
1½ teaspoons finely chopped
fresh tarragon leaves
Half of a small lemon

The scallop is one of the ocean's most divine creatures: meaty, briny, and delicate all at once. When you visit your fishmonger, ask if scallop shells are available, too. Once cleaned, the shells become the perfect serving vessels for this dish, rendering it worthy of a Botticelli painting. If you cannot obtain scallop shells, decorative antique shell plates are equally beautiful.

☞ Line a small baking sheet or a large plate with several layers of paper towels. Remove the side muscles from the sea scallops and arrange the scallops in a single layer on the prepared baking sheet or plate. Chill, uncovered, in the refrigerator while you prepare the pea puree and walnut sauce.

☞ In a large saucepan over medium heat, melt 1 tablespoon of the butter. Add the peas and the water and cook, stirring frequently, until warmed through and steamy, 2 to 3 minutes. Transfer the peas and all of the liquid into a blender and blend until very smooth, adding more water, a small splash at a time, if needed to help the mixture blend. The puree will be thick, so you will most likely have to turn off the blender and use a spoon to give the mixture a good stir a couple of times to help move things along. Transfer the pea puree back into the saucepan and season with salt and pepper. Cover with a lid to keep warm.

☞ In a medium saucepan over medium heat, melt the remaining 4 tablespoons / 60g of butter, stirring frequently, until light brown specks *just* start to form and the butter starts to smell nutty, about 5 minutes. Lower the heat slightly, add the walnuts, stirring constantly, until the nuts are toasted and the butter is well browned, about 2 additional minutes. Turn off the heat and stir in the lemon zest. Season with salt and pepper and cover with a lid to keep warm while you sear the scallops.

☞ In a large cast-iron or stainless-steel skillet over high heat, warm the oil until it starts to shimmer and you see the first wisps of smoke. Use enough oil so that the bottom of the skillet

Recipe continues

is coated with a thin layer; this will help the scallops brown nicely.

☞ While the oil is heating, remove the scallops from the refrigerator and liberally season all over with salt and pepper. Use tongs to carefully add the scallops to the hot oil. Cook until the scallops are well browned and caramelized on the first side (do not move the scallops during this time), about 2 minutes. Turn each scallop over and cook until browned and caramelized on the second side, 1 to 2 additional minutes. Transfer the seared scallops to a plate and cover with aluminum foil to stay warm.

☞ If needed, rewarm the pea puree over medium heat until it is warmed through. Coarsely chop the mint leaves (about 1 heaping tablespoon) and fold into the pea puree. Stir the tarragon into the warm browned butter and walnut sauce.

☞ To serve, dollop a generous spoonful of the minted pea puree onto twelve small serving plates or scallop shells, then top with the seared scallops. Drizzle the browned butter walnut sauce on top of each scallop, and finish with a small squeeze of lemon juice. Serve immediately.

SUCKLING PORK BELLY SKEWERS
with Pickled Cherry Tomatoes

Makes about 24 pieces

Kosher salt
Freshly ground black pepper
2 teaspoons packed light brown
   sugar
¾ teaspoon ground coriander
One 2-pound / 900g piece skin-
   on pork belly (about
   1 inch / 2.5cm thick)
Vegetable oil
2 Persian cucumbers
24 Pickled Cherry Tomatoes
   (recipe follows)

Typically, Queen Charlotte likes to present a whole suckling pig as the centerpiece of her luncheon table. But most of us do not have access to whole animals—nor do we have a butcher on staff to prepare and carve the beast. These pork belly skewers are a wonderful way for modern folk to enjoy a porcine course at lunchtime.

☞ In a small bowl, stir together 2 teaspoons salt, several large grinds of black pepper, the brown sugar, and the ground coriander.

☞ Put the pork belly in a large baking dish and pat the skin and meat completely dry. Use the tip of a sharp paring knife to poke holes all over the top of the skin, being mindful to not poke through into the meat. Do this carefully but aggressively because the more holes you poke, the crisper the skin will get. Flip the pork over and rub the spice mixture all over the meat, avoiding the skin. Flip the pork over and sprinkle the skin liberally with salt. Refrigerate, uncovered, for at least 12 hours and up to 48 hours.

☞ When you are ready to cook the pork belly, preheat the oven to 300°F / 150°C.

☞ Line a baking sheet with foil, then top with a wire rack. Lightly grease the wire rack with vegetable oil. Remove the pork belly from the refrigerator and transfer the meat onto the wire rack skin side up. Pat the skin completely dry.

☞ Bake until the pork belly is cooked through and fork-tender with an internal temperature of 180° to 185°F / 82° to 85°C, 2½ to 3 hours. Remove from the oven and pat both the meat and the skin very dry.

☞ Some of the skin will be firm and some parts will still be soft. Use a sharp paring knife to poke the soft parts with

Recipe continues

PICKLED CHERRY TOMATOES
Makes about 3 cups / 720g

12 ounces / 340g rainbow
  cherry tomatoes (about
  2½ cups)
3 garlic cloves, lightly smashed
¾ cup / 175ml champagne
  vinegar
¾ cup / 175ml water
1½ tablespoons sugar
2½ teaspoons kosher salt
2 teaspoons pink peppercorns
1 bay leaf

Use the tip of a paring knife to poke a very small hole at the bottom of each tomato, then transfer to a large heatproof jar or medium bowl along with the smashed garlic.

In a small saucepan over medium heat, stir together the champagne vinegar, water, sugar, 2½ teaspoons salt, the pink peppercorns, and bay leaf. Cook, stirring frequently, until the sugar and salt dissolve and the mixture is warm but not hot, about 3 minutes. If the brine is too hot, it will make the tomatoes mushy.

Pour the warm brine over the cherry tomatoes and garlic and stir to combine. Cool at room temperature for 30 minutes, then cover the tomatoes and chill in the refrigerator for at least 24 hours and up to 7 days. The pickled flavor of the tomatoes gets stronger the longer they sit in the brine; after the first few days, the tomatoes will also start to get softer, which may make them harder to skewer.

additional holes. Fill a large high-sided skillet with ¼ inch / 6mm of vegetable oil. Put the pork belly, skin side down, into the cold skillet and oil and turn the heat to medium. Slowly heat the oil until it starts to lightly bubble around the pork, then continue to cook gently until the skin is puffed, lightly browned, and very crispy, 8 to 12 minutes of total cooking time. Use tongs to move the pork belly around in the skillet as needed to ensure the skin becomes crisp evenly. The timing for this will depend heavily on your stove top.

☞ Use a long slotted metal spatula and tongs to carefully transfer the pork belly back onto the same wire rack it was roasted on and cool for 15 minutes.

☞ As the pork is cooling, cut off the two ends of the Persian cucumbers, then use a mandoline or a peeler to shave the cucumbers lengthwise into very thin long pieces, about 24 total.

☞ After the pork has cooled slightly, use a serrated knife to cut the pork belly into ¾-inch / 2cm cubes, about 24 total. Use a sharp metal skewer or paring knife to poke a small hole into the center of the skin on top of each piece of pork; this will make it easier to place the pork onto cocktail skewers. Thread each piece of pork onto a cocktail skewer along with a pickled cherry tomato and a cucumber slice. Transfer to a platter and serve.

SUMMER PUDDINGS

with Mixed Berries and Fresh Whipped Cream

Makes 8 servings

1 pound / 450g blackberries (about 3 heaping cups), plus additional for garnish

1 pound / 450g strawberries, stemmed and sliced ¼ inch / 6mm thick (about 3 heaping cups), plus additional thinly sliced for garnish

½ to ⅔ cup / 100 to 130g granulated sugar (depending on the sweetness of your berries)

Kosher salt

1 cup / 240ml black currant juice

¼ cup / 60ml water

1 to 2 tablespoons fresh lemon juice (optional)

28 slices thinly sliced sturdy white sandwich bread

1 cup / 240ml cold heavy cream

2 tablespoons confectioners' sugar

Special Equipment: Eight 8-ounce / 225g tapered ramekins or bowls

This dessert is a tribute to one of Queen Charlotte's great success stories: the Duke and Duchess of Hastings, whose love match she considers her own personal triumph. Nobody has a keener eye for fashion than the queen, who quickly noticed how marvelously the Duke of Hastings wears the color red. The duchess, by contrast, is at her most ethereal when she dons a pale, shimmering blue—a color the queen has noticed many Bridgertons wearing well. This violet-hued confection is the queen's way of slyly celebrating the union of two impeccable (and impeccably dressed) houses.

☞ Line the inside of eight 8-ounce / 225g tapered ramekins or bowls with plastic wrap, leaving at least a 1 inch / 2.5cm overhang on all sides.

☞ In a large bowl, combine the blackberries, strawberries, granulated sugar, and a pinch of salt. Set aside at room temperature until the sugar dissolves and the berries are juicy, about 15 minutes, stirring occasionally.

☞ Transfer the macerated berries and all of the juices into a large saucepan along with the black currant juice and water. Turn the heat to medium and warm gently, stirring occasionally, until the mixture just starts to lightly bubble, about 10 minutes. You want the fruits to soften but still hold their shapes and be vibrant in color. Taste the syrup; it should be sweet with a touch of tartness from the berries. If you would prefer it more tart, stir in the lemon juice; start with 1 tablespoon and add more to taste. Place a large strainer over the same bowl that you used to macerate the fruit and strain berries. Cool both the fruit and syrup at room temperature.

☞ Meanwhile, measure the top and bottom of one of the ramekins or bowls and choose round cutters that match their size (or use an alternative, such as a round drinking glass). Use a large cutter to cut out eight rounds from eight bread slices and place onto a baking sheet. Use a smaller cutter to cut out eight small rounds from eight additional bread slices and place onto the baking sheet. If desired, save any bread scraps to make bread crumbs.

☞ For the remaining twelve bread slices, use a serrated knife to cut away the crusts, then cut each slice into four even squares (about 1½ inches / 4cm square). Place the squares on the baking sheet with the bread rounds.

☞ Quickly dip one of the small bread rounds into the cooled fruit syrup, then place on the bottom of one of the ramekins or bowls. Quickly dip one of the bread squares into the syrup, then place on the side of the ramekin (on top of the small bread round). Repeat this with five additional bread squares and work in a circular pattern to arrange the bread pieces evenly around the sides of the ramekin, overlapping the bread slightly so that there are no gaps. Spoon one-eighth of the cooked fruit into the center of each ramekin, then use a spoon to lightly press down on the fruit to compact it. Quickly dip a large bread round into the syrup and place on top of the fruit.

☞ Seal the top of each summer pudding with the overhanging plastic wrap. Place the ramekins on a baking sheet, then place a weight on top of each to weight it down and compact it (small cans work well). Refrigerate for at least 6 hours and up to overnight.

☞ Just before serving, in a medium bowl, combine the heavy cream and confectioners' sugar. Use a whisk to whip until very soft, pillowy peaks form.

☞ Remove the summer puddings from the refrigerator and take off the weights. One by one, remove the plastic wrap from each pudding, then invert the ramekin or bowl onto a small serving plate. Gently tug down on the plastic wrap to help release the pudding, then remove the plastic wrap. Top with large dollops of the whipped cream and garnish with additional berries. Serve immediately.

BLUEBERRY AND ELDERFLOWER CHAMPAGNE PUNCH

Makes 8 to 10 servings

32 to 64 small edible flowers, such as pansies, violas, and/or marigolds

8 ounces / 225g blueberries (about 1½ cups), plus additional for garnish

½ cup / 100g sugar

Pinch of kosher salt

½ cup / 120ml water

1 cup / 240ml elderflower liqueur, such as St-Germain

Two 750-ml bottles dry Champagne or sparkling white wine, chilled

Special Equipment: Two standard ice cube trays (15 to 16 compartments each)

This Champagne drink is a perfect excuse to show off your most stately punch bowl. But if you do not own gorgeous crystal serving ware, fear not. These beautiful ice cubes with edible flowers enshrined within will more than make up for an ordinary serving vessel. Elderflower liqueur is a delicious addition here: It lends a delicate, floral aroma and honeyed sweetness to the drink.

☞ Arrange one or two edible flowers in the bottom of each compartment of two standard ice cube trays, then fill the trays with water. Alternatively, you can make eight to twelve large square ice cubes using larger molds and filling the compartments with assorted edible flowers. For extra-clear ice cubes, use distilled water. Freeze until completely solid.

☞ In a medium bowl, combine the blueberries, sugar, and a small pinch of salt. Stir to combine, then use a fork to mash down on the berries. Set aside to macerate for 15 minutes.

☞ Transfer the macerated berries to a small saucepan over medium heat and add the water. Bring to a gentle simmer and cook, stirring occasionally, until the berries are softened and the syrup is a deep purple, almost magenta, hue, about 10 minutes.

☞ Remove from the heat and strain the berries through a fine-mesh sieve. Use a spoon to stir the mixture to help the fruit expel the syrup. Keep the strainer of spent blueberries over the syrup while it cools (any additional syrup will slowly drip down), then discard the solids.

☞ Rinse out the strainer, then place it over a large punch bowl and strain the syrup again into the bowl (this will ensure that there are no runaway pieces of fruit in your syrup). Add the elderflower liqueur and Champagne. Stir to combine, then add the edible flower ice cubes and additional blueberries to the punch and serve immediately.

LAVENDER LEMONADE

"I YEARN FOR SOMEONE FRESH, SOMEONE UNEXPECTED TO TURN
THIS SEASON ON ITS HEAD." —QUEEN CHARLOTTE

Makes 6 to 8 servings

2 tablespoons plus ½ teaspoon
   dried lavender buds
6 large lemons (about 2 pounds
   / 900g)
1½ cups / 300g plus
   2 tablespoons sugar
6 cups / 1.4L water, plus
   additional to taste
Ice cubes, as needed

Special Equipment: One small
   coffee filter and kitchen twine

Lemonade is a fixture at every respectable gathering, as it is quite unsuitable for unmarried ladies to overindulge in alcoholic spirits. (Quite the opposite is true for their brothers. Indeed, any bachelor you encounter at a ball is likely to arrive three sheets to the wind after a preparatory afternoon at his club.) Propriety notwithstanding, it is a shame that young ladies are so limited in what they are allowed to drink, which is why Queen Charlotte always offers lemonade with a little something extra.

Cook's Note: If you want to omit the homemade candied lemon slices, you can use the lavender syrup right after it's cooled; just make sure to keep the lavender "tea bag" in the syrup while it cools to maximize the floral flavor. Instead of candied lemon, garnish with fresh lemon slices and edible lavender sprigs.

☞ Place 2 tablespoons of the lavender buds into the center of a "junior"-size coffee filter, then completely enclose the lavender by gathering the filter at the top and tying the top of the filter together using kitchen twine. Set the lavender "tea bag" aside.

☞ To make the candied lemon slices, cut one of the lemons crosswise into thin rounds (ideally a touch thinner than ⅛ inch / 3mm thick; about 12 slices total) and remove any seeds. Fill a medium bowl with ice water and set aside. Fill a large saucepan halfway with water, bring to a boil over medium-high heat, then remove from the heat. Lay the lemon slices in the hot water and let sit until the slices soften, about 5 minutes. Drain the lemon slices and transfer to the ice bath. Set aside while you prepare the lavender simple syrup.

☞ In the same saucepan that you used for the lemon slices, combine 1½ cups / 300g of the sugar and 1½ cups / 360ml water. Bring to a simmer over medium heat, about 5 minutes. Add the lavender tea bag, reduce the heat to medium-low, and gently simmer for 10 minutes. Remove and reserve the tea bag, then

Recipe continues

drain the lemon slices and add to the lavender simple syrup. Allow the mixture to come back to a simmer, cover with a lid, and continue to gently simmer until the lemon slices are tender and almost translucent, about 1 hour.

☞ Line a small baking sheet with parchment paper, then use tongs to carefully lift up the candied lemon slices, one at a time (allowing the excess syrup to drip away), and arrange in a single layer on the prepared baking sheet. Set aside and cool at room temperature until the candied lemon slices feel tacky but not wet, about 24 hours.

☞ Return the reserved lavender tea bag to the saucepan with the hot syrup and cool completely at room temperature. Transfer the cooled syrup (along with the lavender tea bag) into a jar or storage container and cool in the refrigerator while the candied lemon slices dry out.

☞ Once the candied lemon slices are ready, juice the remaining five lemons (you should have about 1 cup / 240ml). Remove and discard the lavender tea bag, then put the syrup into a large pitcher along with the lemon juice and remaining 4½ cups / 1.06L of water. Stir to combine and add more water depending on your preference.

☞ In a small bowl, combine the remaining 2 tablespoons of sugar and ½ teaspoon of lavender buds. In batches, toss the candied lemon slices in the lavender sugar, then return to the baking sheet.

☞ Pour the lavender lemonade into glasses filled with ice, garnish with one or two candied lemon slices, and serve.

Addressing Royalty and Nobility

If you have to *ask* about the rules that govern English society, then you are not a true member of the ton. But for those of us who were not born with a title or an ancient lineage, the English class system is quite inscrutable. How should you behave if you are presented to a king or queen? Is an earl ranked higher than a baron? And what exactly is a viscount, anyways?

The most important rule for mixing and mingling in high society is that you should *never* approach a stranger whose station is higher than your own. A higher-ranking person may approach someone they do not know, but not vice versa. This is why it is helpful to have a powerful champion, such as Lady Danbury, to facilitate introductions on your behalf.

If you are brought before a king or queen, first you must pay homage. For men, a neck bow (from the head only) is appropriate; women are expected to do a small and graceful curtsy. Address the king and queen as "Your Majesty" and subsequently "Sir" and "Ma'am." Princes and other male members of the royal family are first "Your Royal Highness" and thereafter "Sir"; princesses and other female royals are "Your Royal Highness" and then "Ma'am."

Address a ducal couple as "Duke" or "Duchess" or "Your Grace" in speech; "His Grace the Duke of Hastings" and "Her Grace the Duchess of Hastings" in writing.

A marquess and marchioness would be the "Most Honorable the Marquess and Marchioness of Ashdown" in writing, but "Lord and Lady Ashdown" in person. When writing to an earl or countess, address him as the "Right Honorable Earl

A bow is made on entering or exiting a room, upon meeting someone one wants to acknowledge, and at the start and end of a dance.

of Lindsay" and her as the "Countess of Lindsay," but in speech, they are "Lord and Lady Lindsay." A viscount is unique in that it does not use "of" after the title; Anthony is simply the "Right Honorable the Viscount Bridgerton" or "Lord Bridgerton" in conversation. A baron or baroness may be referred to by a place-name or family name (the Baron of XX or simply Baron Featherington) and should be called "lord" or "lady."

The eldest unmarried daughter of a household is called only by her last name; for example, "Miss Sharma." Her younger sisters are called by their first and last names: "Miss Edwina Sharma." The same is true of sons. While his father was alive, Anthony was Mr. Bridgerton and his brothers were Mr. Benedict Bridgerton and Mr. Colin Bridgerton.

The Social Ladder

Monarch

Royalty

Nobility (inherited titles; also known as the peerage)
    Duke
    Marquess
    Earl
    Viscount
    Baron

Gentry (well-regarded families, often with wealth and some degree of power, who are not considered part of the peerage)
    Baronet
    Knight
    Country landowners
    Gentlemen of property but no title

The Rest (artisans, tradespeople, servants, laborers, paupers)

SHERRY COBBLER
with Fruit and Herb Bouquet

Makes 1 cocktail

1 lemon wheel
1 orange wheel
¾ ounce (about
   4½ teaspoons) / 22ml
   Simple Syrup (recipe below)
3 ounces (6 tablespoons) /
   90ml amontillado sherry
Crushed ice
Mint sprig, for garnish
Citrus half wheels, for garnish
Your freshest, most flawless fruit,
   skewered on a cocktail pick,
   for garnish

This cocktail is the perfect early-afternoon refreshment. Its base ingredient, sherry, is a fortified wine and therefore lower-proof than distilled spirits such as whiskey or gin, meaning you can enjoy more than one without embarrassing yourself in front of Her Majesty.

Do not be shy when it comes to the garnish; with Sherry Cobblers, more is more. Ripe summer berries, your orangery's finest citrus, and fragrant herbs—all are welcome here.

☛ Add the lemon wheel, orange wheel, and simple syrup to a cocktail shaker and muddle. Add the sherry, fill the shaker with ice, and shake until chilled. Strain into a wineglass or Collins glass filled with crushed ice. Wedge the mint sprig and citrus half wheels in between the ice and the edge of the glass, then add your fruit skewer and serve with a straw.

SIMPLE SYRUP

1 part sugar
1 part water

☛ Combine the sugar and water in a medium saucepan and bring to a simmer, stirring occasionally until the sugar dissolves. Let cool before using. Store airtight in the refrigerator for up to 1 month.

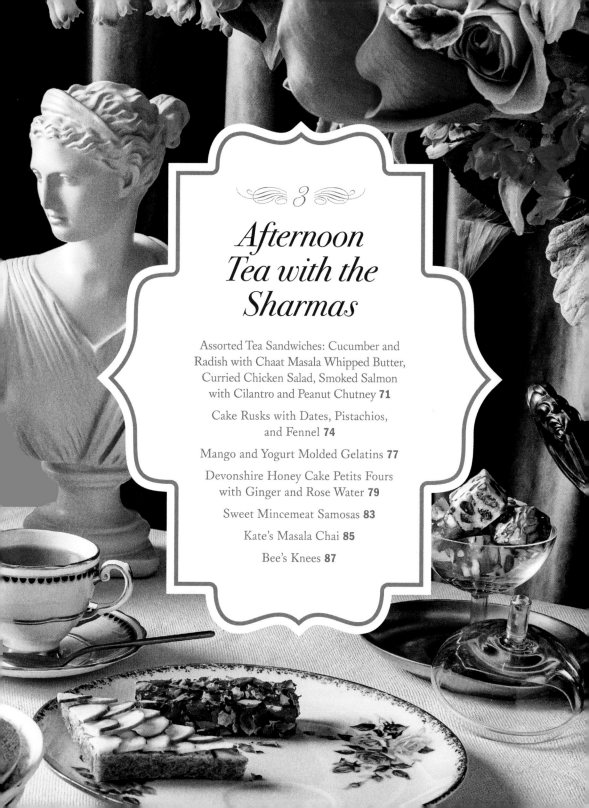

3

Afternoon Tea with the Sharmas

Regardless of what you think about the beverage itself, it is hard to deny the charms of the English tea party. Afternoon tea represents English hospitality at its finest, whether your preparations are modest (a single cup and a slice of cake to share with a dear friend) or grand (your finest china; silver trays with enough sandwiches to feed a small army—or one male Bridgerton).

Although she despises English tea, the Viscountess Kate Bridgerton, née Sharma, cannot fault the ritual that accompanies it. The rules of polite English society can be limiting for women, but afternoon tea is one of the rare venues where Lady Kate knows she can share her true opinions, without having to worry about the prying eyes and ears of the ton. Without tea parties, Lady Kate often wonders whether women would have the opportunity for any meaningful conversation at all.

The recipes in this chapter are full of character—and our hope is that your tea party will be full of characters, too. It doesn't matter if you have a fine porcelain teapot or artfully hewn wooden tea caddy, so long as you are surrounded by interesting people with a healthy appetite for food and discussion.

67

Tea Party

The English obsession with tea is well known and well documented. But what many Brits won't tell you is that the secret to a successful tea has little to do with the drink and everything to do with the quality of the conversation. Invite people you adore and haven't seen in a while for a thoughtful and delicious catch-up.

DÉCOR

Create a space that is intimate and conducive to repartee. If you won't be seated around a table, try to ensure that your guests are sitting roughly in a circle, and close enough so that no one has trouble hearing the banter. Though you can serve tea in anything from vintage bone china to contemporary ceramic mugs, use cups and saucers to summon the spirit of *Bridgerton*. You may have a matching tea set, complete with a sugar bowl and creamer. If not, a quick trip to the local thrift store can yield a bevy of tea-worthy dishware. An eclectic collection of tiny silver spoons will complete the picture. Work in a floral arrangement—perhaps a low bouquet of hydrangeas and peonies that invoke a sun-drenched summer garden, or a delicate nosegay of early spring flowers like daffodils, tulips, and forget-me-nots.

FOOD + DRINK

Learn the art of brewing and serving tea on page 73. Set out small pitchers of cream and your preferred milks, a plate of sliced lemon, and a sugar bowl heaped with lumps of raw sugar. Offer two or three handheld delicacies, starting with savories (such as Tea Sandwiches, page 71) and ending with sweets (Devonshire Honey Cake Petits Fours, page 79). If you have a three-tier serving tray, arrange the savory dishes on the bottom and the sweet ones above it.

Is high tea a fancier version of afternoon tea? Quite the opposite. In England, high tea was originally a substantial meal, served to workers in the late afternoon or early evening. It was often served on high tables or countertops, thus its name. High tea was characterized by hearty, savory food rather than the flaky confections of afternoon tea.

ASSORTED TEA SANDWICHES

Makes 16 pieces each

CUCUMBER AND RADISH WITH CHAAT MASALA WHIPPED BUTTER

¾ cup / 110g unsalted whipped butter, at room temperature

1 tablespoon chaat masala, plus additional to taste

Kosher salt

8 thin slices whole-grain sandwich bread, crusts removed

2 large Persian cucumbers (about 6 ounces / 170g), sliced into very thin rounds (about 1⅓ cups)

6 radishes (about 6 ounces / 170g), sliced into very thin rounds (about 1⅓ cups)

CURRIED CHICKEN SALAD

2 bone-in, skin-on chicken breasts (about 1½ pounds / 680g)

1½ teaspoons unrefined virgin coconut oil

Kosher salt and freshly ground black pepper

⅓ cup / 80g mayonnaise

⅓ cup / 80g whole milk thick Indian-style yogurt (see Cook's Note, page 77)

3 tablespoons spicy or hot mango chutney

1 tablespoon plus 1 teaspoon Madras curry powder

With each passing year, the time between luncheon and dinner stretches ever wider in the most sociable houses of the ton. Especially on the evening of a ball, a lady is lucky if she enjoys her final meal before one o'clock in the morning. For this reason, Kate Bridgerton always enjoys several tea sandwiches in the afternoon to fortify her until dinner—whenever that may be.

☞ **FOR THE CUCUMBER AND RADISH WITH CHAAT MASALA WHIPPED BUTTER:** In a large bowl, combine the whipped butter and chaat masala and stir until well combined and smooth. Season to taste with more chaat masala and/or salt. Spread a slightly heaping tablespoon of butter onto a bread slice, then layer alternating and overlapping cucumber and radish slices on top of the butter. Use a serrated knife to cut each open-faced sandwich in half diagonally. Transfer to a platter and serve.

☞ **FOR THE CURRIED CHICKEN SALAD:** Preheat the oven to 375°F / 190°C.

☞ Place the chicken breasts on a sheet pan, rub the skin with the coconut oil, and sprinkle liberally with salt and pepper. Roast until an instant-read thermometer inserted into the thickest part of one of the chicken breasts registers 165°F / 75°C, about 30 minutes. Transfer the chicken to a cutting board and cool until the chicken is warm but no longer steaming hot, about 30 minutes. Remove the skin and bones, then finely dice the meat. Transfer the chicken to a bowl and chill in the refrigerator until completely cooled. Alternatively, you can use 3 cups / 450g of diced precooked chicken.

☞ In a medium bowl, combine the mayonnaise, yogurt, mango chutney, and curry powder. Whisk to combine, then stir in the chilled chicken, celery, green onions, and cashews. Fold in the grapes and season with additional salt and pepper. Divide the chicken salad among eight bread slices. Spread the chicken salad out to cover the bread completely, then top with eight additional bread slices. Use a serrated knife to cut each

Recipe and ingredients continue

½ cup / 65g finely diced celery

⅓ cup / 25g sliced green onions

¼ cup / 35g coarsely chopped roasted salted cashews

½ cup / 80g small seedless black grapes, quartered

16 thin fruit-and-nut sandwich bread slices (or substitute thinly sliced brioche), crusts removed

SMOKED SALMON WITH CILANTRO AND PEANUT CHUTNEY

¼ cup / 30g raw shelled peanuts

1 large bunch cilantro (about 2½ ounces / 75g), tough lower stems discarded and leaves and soft stems coarsely chopped (about 2 packed cups)

1 garlic clove, finely grated

1 green bird's-eye chile, thinly sliced

2 tablespoons fresh lime juice, plus additional to taste

2 tablespoons water, plus additional as needed

Pinch of sugar (optional)

Kosher salt

16 thin white or wheat sandwich bread slices, crusts removed

4 ounces / 115g whipped cream cheese

8 ounces / 225g smoked salmon

sandwich in half diagonally or cut into quarters. Transfer to a platter and serve.

☞ **FOR THE SMOKED SALMON WITH CILANTRO AND PEANUT CHUTNEY:** In a small skillet over medium heat, lightly toast the peanuts until browned in spots, 6 to 8 minutes, shaking the skillet occasionally. Transfer to a small bowl and cool completely.

☞ In a blender, combine the cooled peanuts, cilantro, garlic, chile, lime juice, water, sugar (if using), and a large pinch of salt. Blend until smooth, stopping and giving the ingredients a good stir every now and then. The chutney will be thick, but you can add a small splash of additional water to help move things along in the blender. Transfer to a small bowl and season with more salt and lime juice, if desired.

☞ Cut each bread slice in half to make two rectangles. Spread half a tablespoon of whipped cream cheese onto one of the bread slices, then swirl 1 teaspoon of the chutney into the cream cheese. Top with a layer of smoked salmon (about ½ ounce / 15g), then top with a second bread slice. Repeat to make sixteen tea sandwiches total. Transfer to a platter and serve. Store any leftover cilantro and peanut chutney in an airtight container in the refrigerator for up to 5 days.

KATE:
Might I offer you some refreshment, Mr. . . . .

MR. BROOKES:
*Brookes. Only if you insist. I mean, it would be churlish to refuse.
Tea, three spoons of sugar, and perhaps some sandwiches, too.
Thank you.*

How to Prepare a Proper Pot of Tea

☞ Fill a kettle with freshly drawn cold water and bring to a boil.

☞ If desired, you may warm the teapot by pouring a bit of hot water into it. Swirl the water around, then discard it.

☞ While the water is coming to a boil, add loose tea to your teapot: 1 to 2 teaspoons per cup of water.

☞ As soon as the water reaches a boil, pour it over the loose tea in the teapot.

☞ Allow the tea to steep—timing is determined by the type of tea and your guests' taste preference (steep longer for a more assertive flavor; shorter for a milder tea).

Suggested Brew Times

White	1 to 2 minutes
Green	2 minutes
Oolong	2 to 3 minutes
Herbal	3 to 4 minutes
Red	3 to 4 minutes
Chai	3 to 5 minutes
Black	3 to 5 minutes

Tea Etiquette

Politeness dictates that the hostess or host will ask each guest how they take their tea (with sugar, with milk, or with lemon) and prepare each cup before placing it on a saucer and handing it to the guest. Always prepare and pass one cup at a time.

When drinking, hold your teacup by its handle, rather than wrapping your hand around the whole cup (this isn't a coffee mug, after all). Simply grasp the handle with your thumb and forefinger, bearing in mind that a protruding pinkie would immediately mark you as a rube. Return your cup to its saucer after every sip.

It should go without saying: Sip your tea rather than gulping or slurping it, or you may find your manners mocked in the next issue of *Whistledown*.

CAKE RUSKS

with Dates, Pistachios, and Fennel

Makes about 24 pieces

1 cup / 140g all-purpose flour
1¼ teaspoons baking powder
½ teaspoon kosher salt
½ cup / 100g granulated sugar
1 tablespoon finely grated fresh
  orange zest
⅛ teaspoon ground turmeric
¾ teaspoon whole fennel seeds,
  coarsely crushed
½ cup / 110g (1 stick) unsalted
  butter, at room temperature,
  plus additional for greasing
2 whole eggs plus 1 egg yolk, at
  room temperature
6 soft medjool dates (about
  4 ounces / 115g), pitted and
  coarsely cut into ½-inch /
  1.3cm pieces
½ cup / 70g raw shelled
  pistachios, coarsely chopped
3 tablespoons turbinado sugar

These twice-baked cakes—which may remind some readers of their Italian cousin, biscotti—are a teatime classic in many parts of India. Dip them in fragrant chai (page 85), a London Fog latte (page 33), or whatever piping-hot potable graces your tea table.

☞ Preheat the oven to 350°F / 175°C. Grease an 8-inch / 20cm square cake pan with butter, line with parchment paper, then grease the paper and set aside.

☞ In a medium bowl, whisk together the flour, baking powder, and salt. Set aside.

☞ In a large bowl, combine the granulated sugar, orange zest, turmeric, and fennel seeds. Use your fingers to rub the zest and seeds into the sugar until it resembles wet sand. Add the ½ cup of butter and beat with an electric hand mixer set at medium-high speed until the mixture is fluffy, about 5 minutes. Beat in the eggs, one at a time, and blend until smooth. Add the egg yolk and blend until smooth. Add the flour mixture and stir with a rubber spatula until just combined. The batter will be thick. Fold in the medjool dates and pistachios.

☞ Spoon the batter into the prepared cake pan, smooth out the top, and sprinkle with the turbinado sugar. Bake until a wooden skewer inserted into the center of the cake comes out clean, 25 to 30 minutes. Cool the cake in the pan for 10 minutes, then invert, remove the parchment paper, and cool completely on a wire rack.

☞ Reduce the oven temperature to 300°F / 150°C. Line a large baking sheet with parchment paper and set aside.

☞ Use a serrated knife to cut the cake in half, then cut each cake half crosswise into ½-inch / 1.3cm thick strips. Arrange the cake slices cut side up on the prepared baking sheet and bake for 20 minutes, then gently flip each strip over. Continue baking until the cake strips feel dry to the touch and are lightly browned in spots, 10 to 20 additional minutes. Remove from the oven and cool on the hot baking sheet for 5 minutes. Transfer to a wire rack and cool completely before serving. The cake rusks will crisp even more as they cool.

MANGO AND YOGURT MOLDED GELATINS

Makes 6 to 12 servings (depending on size)

Vegetable oil, for greasing
¼ cup / 60ml cold water
1 tablespoon powdered gelatin
½ cup / 120ml coconut milk
¼ cup / 50g sugar
¼ teaspoon loose saffron threads, plus additional for garnish
12 ounces / 340g chopped peeled ripe Alphonso mangoes (about 2 cups), plus additional sliced mango for garnish
½ cup / 120g plain whole-milk, thick Indian-style yogurt (see Cook's Note)
Edible flowers for garnish

Special Equipment: Six 4-ounce or twelve 2-ounce metal gelatin molds, ramekins, or custard cups

These beautiful golden gelatins get their vibrant hue from the addition of saffron, a spice harvested from a particular species of crocus flower. Sir Philip Crane, husband of the former Miss Marina Thompson, is a noted botany enthusiast and would have much to add about the singularity of saffron. But for our purposes, it is enough to say that it adds a subtle warmth to this sweet and rich dessert.

Cook's Note: Indian-style yogurt is available at Indian grocery stores. If you cannot find it, substitute a one-to-one mixture of plain Greek-style yogurt and plain American-style yogurt.

☞ Lightly grease six 4-ounce or twelve 2-ounce metal gelatin molds, ramekins, or custard cups and arrange on a baking sheet.

☞ Pour the cold water into a small bowl, sprinkle the powdered gelatin on top, and stir to combine.

☞ In a second small bowl, stir together the coconut milk and sugar. Use your fingers to lightly crumble the saffron and add to the sweetened coconut milk mixture. Stir to combine, then set aside both the gelatin and coconut milk mixture to bloom for 5 minutes. During this time, the gelatin will absorb the water and the saffron will start to flavor and color the coconut milk.

☞ In a blender, combine the coconut milk and saffron mixture, the chopped mango, and yogurt, and blend until smooth.

☞ Scoop the bloomed gelatin into a small saucepan and warm over low heat, stirring frequently, until melted and smooth, about 2 minutes. Add the gelatin to the mango mixture and blend on high speed for 1 minute.

☞ Pour evenly into the prepared molds, ramekins, or custard cups. Chill in the refrigerator until set, at least 4 hours and up to overnight.

☞ To unmold, use a small paring knife to carefully separate the gelatin from the molds. Fill a wide shallow bowl halfway with hot water. One by one, dip the gelatin molds into the hot water, being careful not to get water over the lip of the mold. Let the mold sit in the water for 5 to 10 seconds, then invert the gelatin onto small serving plates and garnish with sliced fresh mango and edible flowers.

DEVONSHIRE HONEY CAKE PETITS FOURS

with Ginger and Rose Water

Makes 36 to 42 pieces

DEVONSHIRE HONEY CAKE
½ cup / 110g (1 stick) plus
   1 tablespoon unsalted butter,
   cut into pats, plus additional
   for greasing
½ cup / 170g honey
¼ cup / 50g packed light brown
   sugar
1-inch / 2.5cm piece fresh
   ginger, peeled and finely
   grated
2 eggs, at room temperature
1⅓ cups / 185g all-purpose
   flour
1 teaspoon baking powder
½ teaspoon kosher salt
¼ teaspoon baking soda
1½ tablespoons hot water
1½ tablespoons granulated
   sugar
1 teaspoon rose water

HONEY BUTTERCREAM
½ cup / 110g (1 stick) unsalted
   butter, at room temperature
2 tablespoons honey
Pinch of kosher salt
1¼ cups / 150g confectioners'
   sugar
1 to 4 teaspoons milk (optional)
¼ cup / 75g tart fruit jam (such
   as raspberry or sour cherry)
   or lemon curd

These delightful cake morsels, with their pink fondant and rose-petal garnish, look like carefully wrapped birthday presents—almost too good to eat. *Almost.* But after your first bite, which reveals a tender cake layered with honey buttercream and tart fruit jam, any hesitation you may feel about eating such a beautiful confection will be thrown out the window.

If you are pressed for time, you can skip the fondant icing entirely: Simply brush the cake with the rose water syrup and frost it with the honey buttercream.

☛ **FOR THE HONEY CAKE:** Preheat the oven to 350°F / 175°C. Lightly grease a 9-inch / 23cm square baking pan with butter. Line the pan with parchment paper, then grease the parchment paper. Place a fine-mesh strainer over a large bowl and set aside.

☛ In a medium saucepan over medium heat, combine the ½ cup of butter, honey, brown sugar, and ginger. Cook, stirring occasionally, until the mixture comes to a simmer, 5 to 8 minutes. Continue to simmer for 2 minutes, then pour the mixture through the strainer set over a bowl (this will remove any fibrous ginger bits) and set aside to cool for 20 minutes, whisking occasionally. The mixture is ready when it is warm but not steaming hot.

☛ Whisk the eggs into the melted honey mixture until smooth. Sift the flour, baking powder, salt, and baking soda over the honey mixture and whisk until smooth. Pour the batter into the prepared baking pan and spread it out into an even layer. Bake until the cake is golden brown and a wooden skewer or cake tester inserted into the middle comes out clean, 25 to 30 minutes, rotating the baking pan once after 20 minutes.

☛ Cool the cake in the pan for 15 minutes, then invert onto a wire rack. Remove the parchment paper, then carefully turn the cake over and cool completely.

Recipe and ingredients continue

FONDANT ICING

1 small red beet (about
3 ounces / 85g), peeled

2⅔ cups / 320g confectioners'
sugar

6 ounces / 170g white
chocolate, coarsely chopped

¼ cup / 60ml hot water, plus
more if needed

3 tablespoons light corn syrup

Edible rose petals (or other
flowers), for topping

☞ Use a serrated knife to cut away the edges from the cooled cake, then cut the cake in half crosswise. Trim the top of the cake as needed to make it nice and flat. Slice each cake half through the middle to create four thin rectangular pieces.

☞ In a small bowl, whisk together the hot water and sugar until the sugar dissolves, then stir in the rose water. Lay each cake half cut side up and brush the syrup evenly onto the cake pieces. Transfer to a small baking sheet and place in the freezer for 20 minutes.

☞ **FOR THE HONEY BUTTERCREAM:** In a large bowl, combine the butter, honey, and a pinch of salt. Beat with an an electric hand mixer on medium-high speed until light and fluffy, 1 to 2 minutes. Add the confectioners' sugar and beat on low speed until combined. Increase the speed to high and beat until the mixture reaches a thick but spreadable consistency, 2 to 3 minutes, adding milk, a teaspoon at a time, if needed.

☞ Remove the cake pieces from the freezer and divide the frosting between the two bottom halves. Spread the frosting so that it covers the tops of the cake pieces completely. Divide the fruit jam or lemon curd between the top halves of the cake and spread it out evenly. Sandwich the top and bottom cake layers together and lightly press down to adhere the cake pieces together. Place the two 2-layer cakes back onto the baking sheet, then freeze until firm, about 30 minutes.

☞ Remove one of the cakes from the freezer and use a serrated knife to cut into 1¼-inch / 3cm cubes and place them onto a second small baking sheet. Return the cake cubes to the freezer and repeat with the second uncut cake, creating 36 to 42 cubes total. Once all of the cake has been cut into cubes, freeze again until firm, about 30 minutes.

☞ **FOR THE FONDANT ICING:** Place a box grater in a medium bowl and grate the beet on the largest hole of the grater directly into the bowl (this will contain the beet juices). Place a small fine-mesh strainer over a small bowl and transfer the grated beet into the strainer. Use the back of a spoon to press down on the beet to extract as much juice as possible, about 1 tablespoon total. Discard the beet and reserve the juice. Sift the confectioners' sugar into a large bowl. Set a wire rack over a baking sheet and set aside along with the beet juice and confectioners' sugar.

☞ Fill a small saucepan with 1 inch / 2.5cm of water. Bring the water to a boil over medium-high heat, then lower the heat to medium (the water should be actively simmering but not vigorously). Place the white chocolate in a heatproof bowl that fits over the saucepan, then place the bowl on top of the simmering water. Heat the chocolate, stirring frequently, until it is melted, about 3 minutes. Turn off the heat but keep the melted chocolate on the stove top.

☞ Working quickly, add the hot water, corn syrup, and beet juice (1 teaspoon of juice for light pink icing and 3 teaspoons for more of a magenta color), and stir with a spatula until well combined and smooth. Add the melted white chocolate and stir again until smooth. The icing should be thick but pourable with a consistency similar to thick caramel sauce. If the mixture is too thick, stir in hot water, a teaspoon at a time, until you reach that consistency.

☞ Remove four of the cake cubes from the freezer, place one on a fork, and use a spoon to pour the icing over the cube until it is completely covered. Use the tip of a sharp paring knife to poke any air bubbles and cover with more icing if needed. Tap the fork on the edge of the bowl to remove excess icing, then place the cake cube onto the wire rack. After the four cubes are coated, lay edible rose petals onto the top of each, lightly pressing the petals into the soft icing. Repeat the process with the remaining cubes. If at any time the icing gets too thick and becomes hard to pour, turn the heat back on to medium under the saucepan of water and place the bowl of icing on top. Gently heat the icing until it is fluid again. Once all of the petit fours have been coated, set aside at room temperature to set up completely, about 2 hours.

SWEET MINCEMEAT SAMOSAS

Makes 16 pieces

⅓ cup / 55g coarsely chopped
 dried apricots
⅓ cup / 45g dried tart cherries
⅓ cup / 45g golden raisins
¼ cup / 30g dried currants
1 small Gala apple, peeled,
 cored, and finely chopped
 (1¼ cups / 160g)
¼ cup / 55ml brandy
⅓ cup / 75ml fresh orange juice
1 tablespoon finely grated
 orange zest
⅓ cup / 65g packed light brown
 sugar
2 tablespoons plus ½ cup /
 110g (1 stick) unsalted
 butter
½ teaspoon ground cinnamon
¼ teaspoon ground cardamom
¼ teaspoon freshly grated
 nutmeg
¼ teaspoon ground ginger
⅛ teaspoon ground cloves
¼ teaspoon kosher salt
⅔ cup / 80g roasted and
 unsalted slivered almonds,
 coarsely chopped
21 phyllo dough sheets
 (approximately 9 by
 14 inches / 23 by 36cm)
Confectioners' sugar for dusting

This recipe is a lovely hybrid of two regional classics. First is mincemeat pie, an English dish traditionally filled with chopped dried fruit, brandy, and spices. Do not be fooled by the name; mincemeat is often vegetarian, as it is here. Second is the samosa, a fried South Asian pastry most commonly filled with savory ingredients like potatoes, onions, and peas. The version here is simplified by calling for a store-bought phyllo pastry instead of a homemade dough, and it is baked rather than fried. This makes cleanup easier for those of us without a full staff of cooks and maids.

☞ In a large saucepan, combine the apricots, cherries, raisins, currants, apple, brandy, orange juice, orange zest, brown sugar, 2 tablespoons of the butter, the cinnamon, cardamom, nutmeg, ginger, cloves, and salt. Turn the heat to medium, stir to combine, and cook until the butter is melted and the mixture comes to a simmer, about 5 minutes, stirring occasionally. Continue to simmer, stirring occasionally, until the apple is tender and most of the liquid is cooked down to a very thick syrup that clings to the fruit, 20 to 25 additional minutes. Transfer the mincemeat to a medium bowl, stir in the chopped almonds, and cool completely. The mincemeat will thicken as it cools.

☞ Once the mincemeat is cooled, preheat the oven to 400°F / 200°C. Line a baking sheet with parchment paper and set aside.

☞ In a small saucepan over low heat, melt the remaining ½ cup of butter, about 5 minutes. Remove the saucepan from the heat and place it on a trivet or kitchen towel close to where you will be forming the samosas. Lay the phyllo sheets onto a second baking sheet and cover with a barely damp kitchen towel. Carefully lay two of the phyllo sheets on a large cutting board and brush gently with a generous amount of the melted butter. Lay two additional phyllo sheets on top of the first two sheets and brush with more of the melted butter. Use a sharp knife to cut the layered phyllo lengthwise into three equal strips.

Recipe continues

☞ With the longer side of one of the strips facing you, place 1 heaping tablespoon of the cooled mincemeat filling on the right side of the phyllo, leaving about ½ inch / 1.3cm of space around three sides of the filling. Fold the upper right-hand corner of the phyllo downward diagonally over the filling so that it meets the bottom of the phyllo dough and forms a triangle. Fold the triangle over once from right to left so that only the bottom of the filling is left exposed. Fold the triangle upward diagonally, then once more from right to left so that the filling is completely encased in the phyllo. Continue to fold the triangle over diagonally downward and upward until you reach the end of the phyllo strip. Brush the top and bottom of the formed samosa with more of the melted butter and transfer onto the prepared baking sheet. Cover with a couple of layers of barely damp paper towels.

☞ Repeat with the remaining phyllo dough sheets, mincemeat filling, and melted butter until you only have one phyllo sheet left. For the last samosa (a total of 16), brush the final phyllo sheet with butter then cut lengthwise into three long strips. Stack the three strips on top of each other, fill with the last of the mincemeat, and repeat the folding process. This samosa will only have three layers of phyllo dough (instead of four) and that is okay.

☞ Bake until golden brown and crispy, about 20 minutes, rotating the baking sheet once after 10 minutes. Cool on the baking sheet for 15 minutes, then lightly dust with confectioners' sugar and serve the samosas warm.

KATE'S MASALA CHAI

Makes 1 serving

5 whole cloves
6 whole black peppercorns
3 whole green cardamom pods
1 cinnamon stick
One ½-inch piece fresh ginger, sliced into thin rounds
1 tablespoon loose black tea, such as Assam (see Cook's Note)
1 cup / 240ml water
½ to ¾ cup / 120 to 175ml whole milk, coconut milk, or other nondairy milk of your choice
2 to 4 teaspoons sugar

MR. DORSET:
London is a far cry from Bombay. It is where you traveled from, yes?

KATE:
Yes.

MR. DORSET:
I have visited. It is a wondrous place. You must miss it dearly.

KATE:
Oh, every minute of every day. But most especially at teatime.

Although much of the tea consumed in England was grown in India, what we think of as "English tea" is actually a tradition imported from China. The Chinese way of serving tea is to steep the leaves in boiling water, which is how it is prepared in England. In India, by contrast, tea leaves, milk, sugar (or jaggery), and spices, such as ginger and cardamom, are combined at the start and vigorously boiled. There is nothing Kate Bridgerton misses more about her home country than this style of chai. Luckily with this recipe, she can re-create the flavors of her childhood in her new homes of Aubrey Hall and Bridgerton House.

Cook's Note: You can substitute 1 to 2 black tea bags for the loose tea.

☛ In the bowl of a mortar, combine the cloves, black peppercorns, green cardamom pods, and cinnamon stick. Lightly crush the spices with a pestle, then transfer into a small saucepan. Add the ginger, black tea, and water. Turn the heat between medium and medium-high and bring the mixture to a vigorous simmer, about 3 minutes. Cover with a lid, reduce the heat to medium-low, and simmer for an additional 5 minutes.

☛ Remove the lid, pour in the milk and as little or as much sugar as you like, and increase the heat to medium. Warm the tea and milk together until the mixture starts to simmer, 3 to 5 minutes, stirring frequently, then continue to simmer the chai for 1 to 2 additional minutes.

☛ Place a small fine-mesh strainer over a mug and strain the tea into the mug. Discard the solids and serve immediately.

BEE'S KNEES

Makes 1 cocktail

2 ounces / 60ml gin
¾ ounce / 22ml fresh lemon
  juice
¾ ounce / 22ml Honey Syrup
  (recipe below) or Vanilla
  Bean-Honey Syrup
  (page 33)
Lemon peel, for garnish

While most tea party beverages are of the benign, nonintoxicating variety, after a particularly charged game of pall-mall (see page 88), you may find yourself craving something a bit stronger. This cocktail is bright, citrusy, and suitable for sipping while the sun still shines.

☛ Combine the gin, lemon juice, and honey syrup in a cocktail shaker and fill with ice. Shake until chilled, then strain into a coupe glass and garnish with the lemon peel. Serve immediately.

HONEY SYRUP

2 parts honey
1 part hot water

☛ Combine the honey and water in a sealable container and shake until well integrated. Let cool before using. Store airtight in the refrigerator for up to 1 month.

Pall-mall, the Bridgerton Way

KATE:
What exactly are the rules of this game?

DAPHNE:
Pall-mall is less about the rules, more about the goal. Which is, of course, to hit your ball through each wicket. The first player to send their ball through the last wicket wins. Simple enough, though if you are feeling devilish, you can use your turn to knock an opponent's ball as far away from their next wicket as you would like.

EDWINA:
Why waste a turn if the point is to get one's own ball through the wicket?

KATE:
To infuriate your opponent, I gather?

DAPHNE:
Precisely. It is a poor player who plays the game, and a wise one who plays their opponent.

KATE:
I believe I shall rather enjoy this game.

Pall-mall will look familiar to modern readers who have played croquet, as it is the latter's precursor: It arrived from France, where it was called *paille-maille*, in the seventeenth century, and quickly became a favorite among England's fashionable elite.

Although a novice when she first arrived in England, Viscountess Kate Bridgerton took to pall-mall like the proverbial duck to water.

Now, any guest who is lucky enough to be welcomed to afternoon tea by the viscountess is invited (read: required) to partake in the Bridgerton family's preferred pastime.

The rules are simple. A series of iron wickets are laid out in a course, then players must hit wooden balls through with mallets. Whoever completes the course in the fewest strokes wins. Sounds like an easy, idle enter-

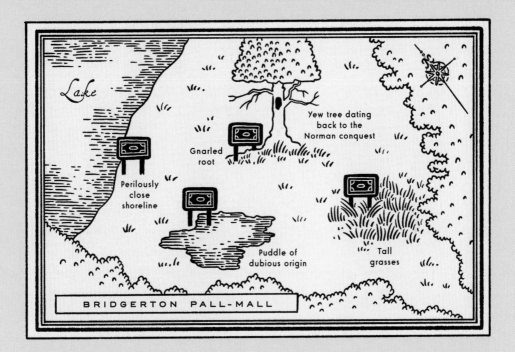

Lake

Yew tree dating
back to the
Norman conquest

Gnarled
root

Perilously
close
shoreline

Puddle of
dubious origin

Tall
grasses

BRIDGERTON PALL-MALL

tainment, does it not? Well, trust the Bridgertons to take a straightforward game and make it more . . . *interesting*.

First, there's the fact that they've never seen the need to set out a regulation course. It is not unusual to find a wicket hidden behind a goat barn or precariously close to a puddle.

Then, there's the uniquely Bridgerton style of play. Whereas your average pall-mall player will use their turn to shoot toward the next wicket, a Bridgerton is just as likely to aim for the ball of whichever sibling is most annoying that day. "Honor and honesty has its time and place," more than one Bridgerton has been heard to say, "but *not* in a game of pall-mall." It is not unusual for a Bridgerton to sacrifice forward progress for the pure pleasure of seeing an opponent stymied. (Your enemy's defeat can taste sweeter than your own success.)

The Bridgerton style is certainly not for all, and it is up to you to determine how cutthroat you'd like your own game to be. Consider your fellow players: Are your guests amiable, innocent daisies? Or are they schemers and cheaters? When in doubt, assume your guests are *not* wolfish tricksters like the Bridgertons. Set out your wickets in a logical progression, ideally in plain sight and, at the very least, in a location that doesn't involve mud, water, or the risk of bodily injury. If you are feeling particularly generous and sportsmanlike, you can even set out a tray of drinks near each wicket, to reward players for their forward progress.

Although the Bridgertons are ruthless competitors, they know they must leave any residual resentment on the field—or face their mother's wrath. And so, every game of pall-mall concludes amicably, with the players shaking hands and making their way indoors to enjoy tea, snacks, and a good-natured ribbing about the events of the day.

4

Dinner at the Featherington Ball

> *"I want luster and glitter
> and gold. I want the best
> of everything."*
> —LADY PORTIA FEATHERINGTON

The best balls start at nine or ten in the evening and hum well into the wee hours—often until sunrise. The *very* best balls require some sort of intervention (servants surreptitiously removing the punch bowl or musicians playing a bit more drearily) to encourage guests to actually leave.

As a hostess, nothing is more mortifying than watching your dance floor empty and guests summon their carriages before the clock has even struck one. The most reliable way to ensure your ballroom stays full and buzzing is to provide ample nourishment. Portia Featherington would rather flee to America than be accused of offering stingy fare at her fêtes. The wine must flow, and the dessert table must be covered with so many trays of sweets that it is impossible to see the tablecloth underneath.

The recipes in this chapter are battle-tested and reveler approved—but do your guests a kindness, dear reader, and serve your supper *before* the rooster crows.

Dinner

Throwing a true Regency-inspired ball is nearly impossible today—it's just so hard to find an apartment with a ballroom, and there aren't enough candlelit chandeliers to go around. Channeling the spirit and flair of the ball, though, is very possible, whether you are hosting a Bridgerton watch party, raucous all-nighter, or special supper with just a few dear friends. This event should be elegant, highly decorated, and thoughtfully staged, so that guests float through the night, buoyed by zippy music, enthusiastic dancing, and just the right amount of bubbly wine.

DÉCOR

Set the scene with a white tablecloth; tall, elegant candles; and more glassware than you think you'll need. (It's a good sign if your guests are having so much fun that they lose track of their beverages.) If possible, use stemware: wineglasses, Champagne flutes, cocktail coupes, and the like have a special way of catching the candlelight and will transform your room into a constellation of glittering glass. If you don't own enough glassware or serving ware, consider renting it—or check your local thrift store for vintage sets. Think about the number of guests you're expecting and the party's flow: If there's any risk it will feel crowded, consider arranging a few drink stations with ice buckets, glasses, and bottles around the perimeter of the room so that everyone isn't crammed into one place. Mix tall candleholders or candelabras with smaller tea lights, so the room feels suffused in light. Add height to your serving table with a structured bouquet of English garden flowers (roses, dahlias, delphiniums) and heap the table with greenery or small, low bouquets to build out the scene. Think about how you want the evening to progress—food first, dancing second?—and plan your playlist accordingly.

FOOD + DRINK

Go tall! Make an impressive, multilevel seafood tower (page 101) for people to pick from. Use a tiered serving tray for your other finger foods. Purchase macarons and fondant to create a whimsical macaron tower (page 118). Let a vintage Regency menu card inspire you to create a custom menu, summarizing the stages of your event (cocktails, dinner, dancing, and coffee and dessert) with style.

Though supper at a proper Regency ball might occur as late as one o'clock in the morning, you might prefer to get some well-earned—and likely much-needed—rest. Adding time stamps to your menu cards ("Coffee and Dessert at 9 p.m.," for example) will help your guests know roughly when you expect the party to end. Although it is considered rude to start clearing dishes while guests are still eating, it is perfectly appropriate to lower the music and start to clear and stack plates when the party is truly over. To eject the more intransigent guests, you can ask what their plans are for the next day and then indicate that you, too, have some plans that require wrapping things up. If your dear auntie doesn't pick up on the hint, politely ask if you can help her call for a car.

SEAFOOD TOWER

Makes 6 to 8 servings

ROASTED SHRIMP COCKTAIL WITH MARIE ROSE SAUCE

2 pounds / 900g extra-jumbo (16 to 20-count) shrimp, peeled, deveined, and tail on

2 tablespoons extra-virgin olive oil

Kosher salt and freshly ground black pepper

1 egg yolk, at room temperature

1 tablespoon fresh Meyer lemon juice, plus additional to taste

¼ teaspoon cayenne pepper

¾ cup / 175ml neutral oil, such as grapeseed oil

3 tablespoons ketchup

1 teaspoon Worcestershire sauce

2 to 4 dashes hot sauce, such as Tabasco

OYSTERS WITH CHAMPAGNE AND APPLE MIGNONETTE

One 750-ml bottle dry Champagne, chilled

2 tablespoons minced shallot

2 tablespoons finely chopped unpeeled Granny Smith apple

⅓ cup / 80ml apple cider vinegar

¼ teaspoon sugar

Kosher salt and freshly ground black pepper

12 to 16 freshly shucked oysters

Crushed ice for serving

The taller the tower of hors d'oeuvres, the closer it is to God—or so says Portia Featherington. "Understated" is simply not a word in her vocabulary, so this seafood tower has not one, not two, but *three* different components.

In your own home, you need not be quite so elaborate. Your guests will be very happy with even just one of these delectable recipes. Or you could head in the opposite direction and be even more decadent than Lady Featherington: Purchase pre-cooked lobster tails and/or crab legs and add them to the tower along with fresh lemon wedges.

☛ **FOR THE SHRIMP COCKTAIL:** Preheat the oven to 450°F / 230°C.

☛ On a large rimmed baking sheet, toss the shrimp with the olive oil and season with salt and pepper. Spread the shrimp out into a single layer and roast until opaque and cooked through, about 10 minutes. Transfer the roasted shrimp to a platter and cool while you make the sauce.

☛ **FOR THE SAUCE:** In a medium bowl, combine the egg yolk, lemon juice, cayenne pepper, and a large pinch of salt and whisk until well combined and smooth.

☛ Very slowly, drizzle the neutral oil into the bowl with the egg mixture, whisking constantly and vigorously. At the beginning, you want to add the oil nearly drop by drop so that the oil binds with the egg mixture to form an emulsion. Make sure that any oil you add is completely incorporated before adding more. Once you have added nearly half of the oil, increase the speed by which you add the oil, but still add it very slowly and continue to whisk constantly and vigorously. (Alternatively, the sauce can be made in a blender or food processor.)

☛ Once all of the oil has been added and the mixture is very thick and creamy, add the ketchup, Worcestershire sauce, and hot sauce and whisk to combine. Season to taste with salt and additional Meyer lemon juice. Transfer the sauce to a serving bowl and place alongside the cooled roasted shrimp.

Recipe and ingredients continue

HERBY CRAB SALAD

¼ cup / 30g very thinly sliced red onion (long pieces cut in half)

½ cup / 50g very thinly sliced fennel (long pieces cut in half), plus hand-torn fronds for garnish

Zest and juice from 1 large Meyer lemon (2 teaspoons finely grated zest and 3 tablespoons juice), plus additional juice to taste

3 tablespoons extra-virgin olive oil, plus additional for drizzling

Kosher salt and freshly ground black pepper

3 tablespoons coarsely chopped fresh flat-leaf parsley leaves

2 tablespoons coarsely chopped fresh dill

2 tablespoons sliced fresh chives

12 ounces / 340g fresh lump crabmeat, picked through for shells

Crackers, toast points, cucumber slices, endive leaves, and/or radicchio leaves for serving

☛ **FOR THE OYSTERS:** Measure out ¼ cup / 60ml of the Champagne and pour it into a small bowl. Add the shallot, apple, apple cider vinegar, sugar, a pinch of salt, and several large grinds of black pepper. Stir to combine. Place the shucked oysters (still on their bottom shells) on a bed of crushed ice and serve immediately with the mignonette and the remaining chilled Champagne.

☛ **FOR THE CRAB SALAD:** In a small bowl filled with ice water, soak the sliced red onion for 10 minutes. Drain well, pat the onions dry, and transfer to a medium bowl. Add the sliced fennel, lemon zest and lemon juice, olive oil, a large pinch of salt, and several grinds of black pepper and stir to combine. Set aside for 10 minutes to marinate the onions and fennel and soften them slightly. Stir in the parsley, dill, and chives, then fold in the crabmeat. Season with additional salt, pepper, and lemon juice. Transfer to a serving bowl, drizzle with additional olive oil, and garnish with hand-torn fennel fronds. Serve with crackers, toast points, cucumber slices, endive leaves, and/or radicchio leaves.

☛ **TO SERVE:** Any one of these three seafood appetizers would be delicious on its own, but for a true showstopper, arrange the finished dishes and their various accoutrements over crushed ice on a two- or three-tiered seafood tower.

SPICED POMEGRANATE MULLED WINE

with Citrus

Makes 8 to 10 servings

1 large blood orange
1 large Cara Cara orange
Two 750-ml bottles full-bodied and fruity red wine, such as Merlot
½ cup / 120ml brandy
½ cup / 120ml orange liqueur, such as Cointreau or triple sec
1¾ cups / 415ml pomegranate juice
½ cup /185g honey
8 whole cloves
3 cinnamon sticks
2 star anise pods
Pomegranate seeds (arils), for garnish

One of the greatest injustices the ton inflicts on young, unmarried ladies is that they are expected to demurely sip tea or lemonade when out in public. Meanwhile, their married counterparts indulge in this tantalizingly fragrant mulled wine, with beautiful pomegranate seeds and orange slices bobbing on the surface. Be bold, dear reader, and defy convention here. Serve this spiced mulled wine to *all* your guests, regardless of their marital status.

☞ Slice the blood orange and Cara Cara orange into thin rounds. Transfer half of the slices from each orange into a small Dutch oven. Halve the remaining orange rounds into half-moons, cover, and reserve at room temperature for garnish. Add the wine, brandy, orange liqueur, pomegranate juice, honey, cloves, cinnamon sticks, and star anise pods to the Dutch oven. Stir to combine.

☞ Over medium heat, bring the wine mixture to a bare simmer, stirring occasionally, about 30 minutes. Decrease the heat to low, partially cover the Dutch oven with a lid, and cook for 1 additional hour.

☞ Place a fine-mesh strainer over a second pot and strain the mulled wine into the second pot. Discard the solids. Ladle the hot mulled red wine into mugs, garnish with the reserved citrus slices and pomegranate seeds, and serve.

MEAT AND POTATO PIES

Makes 6 pies

PIE DOUGH
4½ cups / 630g all-purpose
   flour, plus more for dusting
2 teaspoons kosher salt
¾ cup / 165g cold beef tallow
   (see Cook's Notes)
4 egg yolks
¾ cup / 175ml plus
   2 tablespoons ice water
1 egg

FILLING
12 ounces / 340g venison or
   beef loin, silver skin removed,
   meat cut into fine (about
   ¼-inch / 6mm) cubes
2¼ teaspoons kosher salt
1½ teaspoons freshly ground
   black pepper
1 medium Yukon gold potato
   (about 5 ounces / 140g),
   peeled and quartered
   lengthwise
½ medium rutabaga (about
   5 ounces / 140g), peeled
   and halved lengthwise
1 small yellow onion (about
   5 ounces / 140g), root
   end removed, peeled and
   quartered
½ cup / 110g (1 stick) plus
   1 tablespoon cold unsalted
   butter, cut into small cubes

Special Equipment: One 6-cup
   nonstick jumbo muffin pan

For the English, no meat is more prized than venison. This is not because it is especially delicious—although many think it is! Rather, venison is considered a luxury because it is *royal*. Since the days of William the Conqueror, it has been illegal to hunt on royal lands without the king's permission. And since most of the wilderness where deer roam is considered royal lands, venison meat is very dear indeed (pardon the pun). If you do not have access to venison, feel free to substitute beef instead.

Cook's Notes: Tallow is made by rendering suet, which typically comes from a cow. Many British recipes use tallow or suet to add a rich flavor to pastries. Tallow is mostly sold grated or pelletized but is sometimes found in solid form. If solid, grate it with a box grater or in a food processor before combining it with the other ingredients. If you prefer, you can substitute equal parts lard or unsalted butter for the tallow in this recipe. Butter has a higher water content, so start by adding ⅔ cup / 160ml ice water instead of the ¾ cup / 175ml, and continue to add water, 1 tablespoon at a time, until the dough comes together.

If you are pressed for time, you can also skip the homemade dough entirely: Use four store-bought pie dough sheets instead. Cut each sheet of dough into rounds as called for in the recipe, gathering and rerolling the dough once if needed.

This recipe can easily be doubled to make a dozen meat pies. In that case, make the dough in two separate batches so as not to overload your food processor. Then form all the dough into four disks and follow the recipe as written.

☛ **FOR THE PIE DOUGH:** In a food processor, combine the flour and 2 teaspoons salt and pulse to blend. Add the tallow and pulse until it resembles coarse meal. Add the egg yolks and pulse 2 to 3 more times until it is just incorporated and the dough turns pale yellow. Drizzle in the ¾ cup plus 2 tablespoons ice water and pulse until the mixture just comes together to form a dough; scrape down the sides of the food processor, if needed, halfway through adding the water to ensure everything evenly combines. It is okay if not all the dough has formed into a ball but it should hold together when pinched. If the dough isn't holding together when pinched, add a

Recipe continues

small splash more of water and pulse again. Transfer the dough to a large piece of plastic wrap and use your hands to bring the dough together. Divide the dough in half and pat into two 1-inch / 2.5cm thick disks. Wrap each disk tightly, then chill in the refrigerator until firm, about 30 minutes or up to overnight.

☞ Line a baking sheet with parchment paper and set aside. If you chilled the dough for 30 minutes, then it should be ready to roll. If it was in the refrigerator for longer and it is really hard, let it sit at room temperature until it is still firm but manageable to roll. Lightly dust a clean work surface and a rolling pin with flour. Roll the first disk into an ⅛-inch / 3mm thick round, turning the dough every time you roll it to ensure it does not stick. Cut the dough into three 5½-inch / 14.3cm rounds and three 6½-inch / 16.3cm rounds. An overturned cereal or soup bowl is usually approximately 5½ inches and a slightly larger prep bowl will work for the 6½-inch / 16.3cm size, if you do not have large round cutters. Take any dough scraps and form them back into a ball, reroll the dough to the same thickness, and continue to cut as needed. Save any excess dough in a ball for decorations. Place the smaller rounds on the prepared baking sheet, cover with plastic wrap, and refrigerate along with any excess dough.

☞ Place a 6-cup nonstick jumbo muffin pan on a flat work surface. Working with one piece of the 6½-inch / 16.3cm rounds at a time, center the dough over one of the muffin cups. Press the dough evenly into the cup, making sure the bottom of the dough is flat against the bottom of the cup and then work your way up, evenly pressing the dough into the sides of the cup. If the dough folds over on itself along the sides, that is okay, just make sure to press it evenly into the cup so that it is the same thickness as the rest of the dough. As you press the dough into the muffin cup, the excess dough will come to the top of the cup; make sure to have at least ¼ inch / 6mm of overhang at the top of the muffin cup. Trim any excess dough that exceeds ½ inch / 1.3cm with a paring knife or kitchen shears. Repeat with the remaining two pieces of dough, then cover with plastic wrap and refrigerate the muffin pan.

☞ Repeat rolling the second disk to cut three additional 5½-inch / 14.3cm rounds and three additional 6½-inch / 16.3cm rounds. Remove the muffin pan from the refrigerator. Line the remaining three muffin cups with the 6½-inch / 16.3 cm rounds and again cover the muffin pan with plastic wrap and

LORD COWPER:
I say, Featherington, I bet you could never find a venison like this in the Americas.

JACK FEATHERINGTON:
There is certainly nothing like English cooking.

refrigerate. Roll the excess dough to a thickness of ⅛ inch / 3mm and cut into decorative shapes (such as flowers or leaves) and refrigerate on the parchment paper–lined baking sheet with the 5½-inch / 14.3cm dough rounds, covered in plastic wrap.

☞ **FOR THE FILLING:** Thoroughly pat dry the venison or beef cubes with a paper towel to remove any excess moisture, then transfer into a medium bowl. Season the meat with 2 teaspoons of the salt and the black pepper and toss to combine. Set aside.

☞ Slice the potato, rutabaga, and onion crosswise on a mandoline into ¹⁄₁₆-inch / 2mm slices. As you cut each vegetable, place each into its own separate bowl.

☞ **TO ASSEMBLE AND BAKE:** Position one rack in the center of the oven and preheat to 375°F / 190°C.

☞ Remove the muffin pan and other pieces of cut dough from the refrigerator. Divide the meat evenly among the six dough-lined cups. Evenly layer the potato slices over the meat, pressing down lightly to evenly pack the meat pies. Repeat with the rutabaga slices, then with the onion slices. Season each muffin cup with the remaining ¼ teaspoon of salt, then evenly scatter the butter cubes on top of the onion slices.

☞ Cover each muffin cup with one of the 5½-inch / 14.3cm dough rounds. Press down lightly on the top of the dough to flatten the filling to the edge of the cup. Press the two edges of the top and bottom dough together against the muffin pan to seal. Next, roll the bottom crust up over the top crust and then fold over every ⅛ inch / 3mm or so to create a pleated design.

☞ Whisk the egg until smooth, then brush the tops of the meat pies with the egg wash. Use a paring knife to cut two very small slits into the top of each pie. While the egg wash is still wet, gently press on any dough decorations to the top of the meat pies to adhere them, ensuring you do not cover any of the vents. Brush the tops of the decorations with egg wash.

☞ Bake the meat pies until the dough is golden brown all over, and the butter starts to bubble up through the vents, about 40 minutes, rotating the baking sheet once after 20 minutes. Remove from the oven and let rest in the pans for 10 minutes. Carefully transfer the hot pies to a wire rack set over a baking sheet and let cool another 20 minutes before serving.

Dance Etiquette

FIRST GENTLEMAN:
Miss Bridgerton, may I request your next dance?

SECOND GENTLEMAN:
Or I might accompany you to fetch some lemonade? You seem parched.

PENELOPE:
How can you tell? Is she wilting?

SECOND GENTLEMAN:
Or punch, if you prefer?

PENELOPE:
A plant pun, if you're wondering.

ELOISE:
Apologies, gentlemen. I regret to inform you that my dance card is already full.

PENELOPE:
Lord Byron? Wellington? Eloise, these names are false!

ELOISE:
I am merely following my sister's valuable advice. She told me that it is of the utmost importance for a lady's dance card to be filled with all of the right names.

For those of us who are not blessed with the gift of rhythm, dancing in public can be a torturous proposition indeed. Now imagine, dear reader, that your marriage prospects—and by extension, your hopes for a happy and comfortable future—depend on your ability to gracefully execute a quadrille. It's enough to make one tremble at the first trill of a violin.

These high stakes mean that the young ladies and gentlemen of the ton take ballroom dancing very seriously. Miss Kate

The Featherington Ball

ORDER OF DANCES

—

SCOTCH REEL
COUNTRY DANCE
COTILLION
QUADRILLE
WALTZ

planned for the evening, in order, with a blank space next to each. Guests collect their dance cards upon arrival. Forward-thinking gentlemen will quickly find their prospective partners and ask them for the honor of a turn—the country dance, for example, or the waltz. If accepted, he will pencil his name next to the agreed-upon dance. It is considered quite rude for a lady to decline an invitation, unless she does not plan to dance for the entire evening.

2.

Debutantes should not dance with the same gentleman more than twice in a row. Unless, of course, they are prepared to entertain not-so-subtle whispers about a forthcoming engagement. "Did you truly dance with the Bridgerton girl? Twice?" Will asks his good friend, the Duke of Hastings, in between punches at their boxing practice. Will is quite rightly shocked that the duke would monopolize the time of such an eligible young lady when he has no intention of marrying her.

3.

The waltz is considered the most intimate dance of all. For this reason, a lady must choose her waltzing partner very carefully. Except under special circumstances (if she is asked by a Prussian prince, for example), a lady should waltz only with a gentleman she knows well.

Sharma went to great lengths to teach her sister, Edwina, the cotillion, quadrille, and waltz because she knew that no gentleman would marry a young lady with two left feet.

Learning the steps of the most fashionable dances is only the beginning. As with all things relating to the Marriage Mart, there are strict rules governing how lords and ladies of the ton should dance together.

1.

If you are hosting a ball, you are expected to lay out dance cards and small pencils for your guests on a table by the entryway. The cards should list every dance

GRILLED LAMB CHOPS
with Pomegranate and Mint Relish

Makes 12 pieces

12 small lamb rib chops,
    frenched (about 2½ pounds
    total) (see Cook's Note)
¼ cup / 60ml extra-virgin
    olive oil
3 garlic cloves, finely grated
1 cup / 150g fresh
    pomegranate seeds (arils)
1 small shallot, finely chopped
1 tablespoon red wine vinegar
½ teaspoon sugar
¼ teaspoon crushed red pepper
    flakes
Kosher salt and freshly ground
    black pepper
6 large fresh mint leaves

According to some scholars, it was not an apple that tempted Eve, but rather a pomegranate. The latter certainly seems more worth the price—what a shame to be banished from the Garden of Eden for something so banal as an apple.

Here, a jeweled pomegranate relish adorns small but succulent lamb chops, an unexpected but brilliant pairing that results in gustatory fireworks. Luckily, there is no need to resist the temptation of this delectable dish.

Cook's Note: Frenching refers to scraping some meat off the bone to create chops that are more easily held by hand. You can ask your butcher to do this for you.

☞ Place the lamb chops in a large bowl or on a baking sheet and rub on all sides with 2 tablespoons of the olive oil and the grated garlic. Set aside to allow the meat to come to room temperature, about 20 minutes.

☞ Meanwhile, in a small bowl, stir together the pomegranate seeds, shallot, red wine vinegar, the remaining 2 tablespoons of olive oil, the sugar, red pepper flakes, and a large pinch of salt. Set the pomegranate relish aside.

☞ Preheat a charcoal grill, gas grill, or cast-iron grill pan to high heat.

☞ In batches, season the lamb chops liberally with salt and pepper and add in a single layer to the hot grill. Cook until deeply charred in spots on the first side, about 2 minutes. Flip the lamb chops over and cook until the second side is deeply charred in spots, about 2 minutes for medium-rare and about 3 minutes for medium doneness.

☞ Transfer the lamb chops to a large platter and let rest for 5 minutes. Coarsely chop the mint leaves and stir into the pomegranate relish. Transfer to a small serving bowl and serve alongside the lamb chops. Alternatively, you can serve the lamb chops with the pomegranate relish spooned on top.

ROASTED HARVEST SQUASH

with Port Wine and Cherry Sauce

Makes 6 servings

2 tablespoons cold unsalted butter

½ small red onion, finely chopped

Kosher salt and freshly ground black pepper

12 ounces / 340g cherries, stemmed, halved, and pitted

⅛ teaspoon ground allspice

½ cup / 120ml ruby port wine

⅓ cup / 80ml red wine vinegar

¼ cup / 85g honey

2 medium delicata squash, about 12 ounces / 340g each

1 small acorn squash, about 1 pound / 450g

2 tablespoons extra-virgin olive oil

Whole fresh flat-leaf parsley leaves for garnish

Every supper table needs a salubrious vegetable dish, especially if you are expected to waltz your way across a ballroom after eating. These elegantly shaped squash are perfect fare for a ball: They're hearty but not so heavy as to inhibit dancing and merrymaking.

☞ In a medium saucepan over medium heat, warm 1 tablespoon of the butter. Add the red onion, season with salt and pepper, and cook, stirring occasionally, until tender, about 5 minutes. Increase the heat slightly, add the cherries, and cook, stirring occasionally, until the cherries are starting to soften and become juicy, about 5 minutes. Stir in the allspice, then add the port wine and red wine vinegar. Bring to a vigorous simmer, and cook, stirring occasionally, until the mixture is reduced by about two-thirds, about 15 minutes. When in doubt, it is better to reduce the sauce more than less. Turn off the heat, then stir in 3 tablespoons of the honey and the remaining 1 tablespoon of butter. Stir until the butter is melted into the sauce, transfer to a medium bowl, then set aside to cool while you prepare the squash. The sauce will thicken as it cools.

☞ Put a rack on the lowest shelf in the oven and place a baking sheet on it. Preheat the oven to 450°F / 230°C.

☞ Cut away the stems from the delicata squash, then cut each squash in half lengthwise. Scoop out the seeds, then cut crosswise into ¾-inch / 2cm thick half-moons. Transfer to a large bowl. Cut away the stem from the acorn squash, then cut the squash in half lengthwise. Scoop out the seeds, then cut into 1-inch / 2.5cm thick wedges. Transfer the acorn squash wedges to the bowl with the delicata squash, drizzle with the olive oil, season liberally with salt and pepper, and toss to combine. Arrange the squash in a single layer on the hot baking sheet.

☞ Roast until the underside of the squash is deeply browned in spots, about 20 minutes. Remove from the oven and carefully

Recipe continues

flip the squash pieces over. Return to the oven and roast until the squash is browned on the second side and very tender, 10 to 15 minutes.

☞ Remove from the oven and cool the squash on the hot baking sheet for 10 minutes. This will help the squash set and will ensure that the pieces stay intact when you remove them from the baking sheet. The sauce should be cooled and slightly thickened at this point. Stir in the remaining 1 tablespoon of honey and season with salt and pepper.

☞ Transfer the roasted squash onto a large platter. Drizzle with some of the port wine and cherry sauce and garnish with whole parsley leaves. Spoon any remaining sauce into a small bowl and serve alongside the squash.

TROPICAL FRUIT ETON MESSES

Makes 8 servings

3 egg whites, at room temperature

½ teaspoon coconut extract

¼ teaspoon kosher salt

⅛ teaspoon cream of tartar

⅔ cup / 130g plus 6 tablespoons / 75g superfine sugar

12 ounces / 340g peeled and finely diced kiwis (about 2 cups)

12 ounces / 340g peeled and finely diced papaya (about 2 cups)

Seeds and pulp (about ½ cup) from 2 large passion fruits (5 to 6 ounces / 140 to 170g)

2 cups / 480ml cold heavy cream

When her cook presented a dessert with the word "mess" in its title, Portia Featherington thought of firing him on the spot. Then she took one bite of this meringue, cream, and tropical-fruit concoction and realized her error. Of course, she didn't *admit* her error to anyone else—she simply smiled and took another spoonful of her delicious mess.

Cook's Note: You can substitute store-bought meringue cookies rather than making your own. You can also make a daintier version of this dessert by dividing the fruit, whipped cream, and meringues among 12 to 16 small serving glasses.

☞ Preheat the oven to 200°F / 95°C. Line a baking sheet with parchment paper.

☞ In the bowl of a stand mixer fitted with a whisk attachment, combine the egg whites, coconut extract, salt, and the cream of tartar. Beat on medium speed until soft peaks form, about 2 minutes. Increase the speed to medium-high and add ⅔ cup / 130g of the superfine sugar, sprinkling in a half tablespoon at a time and waiting 15 to 20 seconds between each addition. Continue beating until all of the sugar has been added, about 5 minutes. Scrape down the sides of the bowl and continue to beat on medium-high speed until the egg whites are glossy, thick, and hold their shape well, about 2 additional minutes. Rub a small amount of the meringue in between your fingers; it is ready if you do not feel any sugar granules. If it is gritty, beat the meringue for a touch longer until it is smooth.

☞ Transfer the meringue to a large pastry bag or plastic storage bag fitted with a large open or curved star tip. Pipe a small amount of meringue in the four corners of the baking sheet and make sure the meringue adheres to the parchment paper; this will ensure that it doesn't lift up while you pipe the rest of the meringue and during baking. Pipe 1½-inch / 4cm wide mounds (about 1½ inches / 4cm tall) onto the baking sheet to make about 32 mounds total. The meringues can be relatively close

Recipe continues

together because they do not spread. Also, they do not have to be perfectly shaped since they will be broken up in the finished dessert. Bake the meringues for 3 hours, then turn off the oven, leaving the meringues to cool gradually in the oven until they are dry to the touch and the bottoms release easily from the parchment paper, about 2 hours. Store the meringues in an airtight container at room temperature for up to 5 days. (They will become sticky if they are exposed to the air for too long.)

☞ When you are ready to serve, in a medium bowl, combine the kiwis, papayas, passion fruits, and 2 tablespoons of the remaining superfine sugar. Stir until combined, then set aside until the sugar dissolves and the fruit is juicy, about 10 minutes. Meanwhile, in the bowl of a stand mixer fitted with a whisk attachment, combine the heavy cream and the remaining 4 tablespoons of superfine sugar and whip on medium speed until soft peaks form, about 3 minutes.

☞ Remove the cooled meringues from the oven and use a serrated knife to cut each into 4 to 6 pieces (it is okay if some of the pieces crumble).

☞ In each of eight small serving cups or bowls, layer 3 tablespoons of the whipped cream, 2 heaping tablespoons of the fruit, and a small handful of the meringue pieces. Repeat this once more, then finish with a couple of spoonfuls of whipped cream and more fruit. Serve.

How to Construct a Macaron Tower

In the years following the 1789 revolution, many of France's finest chefs landed on English shores after fleeing Madame la Guillotine. The best were quickly scooped up by English nobles and employed in their kitchens. The prince regent himself paid an extraordinary sum to enlist the renowned chef Marie-Antoine Carême, who worked for several months at the prince's London residence, Carlton House.

The surest sign that a household has a French confectioner on staff is if you are greeted by a tray of French sweets upon arrival. Macarons are particularly popular but notoriously finicky to make, which is why we encourage readers who do *not* have a French chef on staff to simply purchase macarons from a reputable baker.

Even if your macarons are store-bought, you should still display them with aplomb. Consider constructing a *tour macaron* (macaron tower) to showcase the delicate confections. If, upon seeing your artful arrangement, your guests assume that you have a pâtissier in your employ, there is no need for you to correct them.

You Will Need:
- Fondant, purchased from a craft store, kitchen supply store, or some well-stocked grocery stores
- Styrofoam cone, purchased from a craft store (it's entirely up to you how tall you wish yours to be)
- Corn syrup
- Pastry brush
- Confectioners' sugar
- Meringue powder
- Macarons

1.

First, assemble the base for your tower. Roll the fondant into a very thin sheet that is as tall as your cone. Using a pastry brush, paint one side of the fondant with corn syrup (this will help it adhere to the Styrofoam). Bring your cone to the fondant and press down so one side adheres. Roll the cone, thereby wrapping it in fondant. Once the cone is fully wrapped, trim the excess fondant from the top, bottom, and seam. Use your fingers to press the seam together. If desired, you can use corn

syrup to affix the base of your cone to its serving plate or stand.

2.

Next, make your edible adhesive. Royal icing works best for this. In a large bowl, combine 1 pound / 455g (about 3½ cups) confectioners' sugar and 2 tablespoons meringue powder. Add 5 tablespoons / 75ml water and beat with an electric mixer on medium-high speed, adding up to 1 tablespoon more water, if needed, until the icing is thick and glossy, about 2 minutes. (If you like, you can add food coloring to make the icing match the color of your macarons.) Transfer the icing to a piping bag or a plastic storage bag and cut a small opening in one corner of the bag.

3.

Now it is time to assemble your tower. Pipe a dollop of royal icing onto the back of one of your macarons. Starting from the bottom of your cone, affix the macaron by pressing gently. Work one row at a time, from the bottom of the cone to the top. You will have to play with the spacing of the macarons a bit to ensure that each row fits full macarons and the gaps in between each macaron are minimal. If the macarons start to slip, wait a few minutes between rows to allow the icing to dry completely.

4.

When you get to the top, affix a single macaron, lying flat, to conceal the tip of the cone, if desired.

PROFITEROLES

with Pink Peppercorn Pastry Cream and Champagne Strawberries

Makes about 60 pieces

PINK PEPPERCORN PASTRY CREAM

1½ cups / 360ml whole milk
1½ cups / 360ml heavy cream
⅔ cup / 130g granulated sugar
½ teaspoons kosher salt
¼ cup / 35g plus 1 tablespoon
   cornstarch
5 egg yolks, at room
   temperature
2 teaspoons vanilla extract
2½ tablespoons cold unsalted
   butter, cut into small cubes
1 tablespoon pink peppercorns,
   lightly crushed

CHOUX PASTRY

¾ cup / 175ml water
½ cup /120ml whole milk
½ cup / 110g (1 stick) plus
   2 tablespoons unsalted
   butter, cut into 8 to 10 pats
1½ teaspoons granulated sugar
¼ teaspoon kosher salt
1¼ cups / 175g all-purpose
   flour
5 large eggs, at room
   temperature

If you notice party guests lingering by the dessert table instead of dancing or chatting with potential suitors, do not assume they are hopeless wallflowers. It could just be that they've come under the spell of these enchanting cream puffs, with their decadent filling of Champagne-soaked strawberries. It's rare to meet a conversationalist who is more diverting than a good profiterole.

Cook's Note: This recipe makes enough profiteroles for a large crowd, but if you do not want to make them all at once, you can save the choux pastry for later use. The dough can be refrigerated for up to 3 days or wrapped very well and frozen for up to 3 months. If frozen, thaw the dough overnight in the refrigerator, then pipe and bake per the recipe's original instructions.

☞ **FOR THE PASTRY CREAM:** In a medium saucepan over medium heat, stir together the milk, 1 cup / 240ml of the heavy cream, ⅓ cup / 65g of the granulated sugar, and the salt. Warm gently, stirring occasionally, until the sugar completely dissolves, about 10 minutes. Turn off the heat. Place a large fine-mesh strainer over a medium bowl and set aside.

☞ In a large bowl, whisk together the cornstarch, egg yolks, and remaining ⅓ cup / 65g sugar until smooth. While continually whisking, slowly pour in about ½ cup / 120ml of the warm milk mixture and whisk until smooth. Continue whisking and adding ½ cup / 120ml of the warm milk mixture at a time until completely combined and smooth.

☞ Transfer the mixture to the saucepan and turn the heat to medium. Cook, whisking constantly, until the mixture is steamy and thickened to the consistency of very thick pudding, about 20 minutes. Do not rush this process, since you do not want to scorch the milk and cream. Remove from the heat, then whisk in the vanilla extract and butter until smooth and glossy.

☞ Strain the pastry cream through the fine-mesh strainer and use a rubber spatula to help push the cream into the bowl below.

Recipe and ingredients continue

CHAMPAGNE MACERATED STRAWBERRIES

8 ounces / 225g small strawberries, stems removed and berries sliced ⅛ inch / 3mm thick (slices halved if the strawberries are large)

¼ cup / 60ml dry Champagne

2 tablespoons granulated sugar

PINK STRAWBERRY SUGAR

¼ cup / 30g confectioners' sugar

½ ounce / 15g freeze-dried strawberries (about 1 cup)

Stir in the pink peppercorns. Cover with plastic wrap, pressing it directly onto the surface of the pastry cream, and cool at room temperature for 30 minutes before transferring it to the refrigerator to chill, at least 2 hours and up to overnight.

☞ Once the pastry cream is completely chilled, in a large bowl, whip the remaining ½ cup / 120ml of heavy cream either by hand or with an electric hand mixer until stiff peaks form. Push the whipped cream to one side of the large bowl. Remove the pastry cream from the refrigerator and give it a good whisking to loosen it up. Scrape the pastry cream into the large bowl next to the whipped cream. Use a rubber spatula to fold the whipped cream into the pastry cream, then gently stir until combined. Transfer into a piping bag or large plastic storage bag fitted with a large open star tip and store in the refrigerator until you are ready to use it.

☞ **FOR THE CHOUX PASTRY:** Position two racks in the upper and lower center of the oven and preheat to 425°F / 220°C. Line two baking sheets with parchment paper and set aside.

☞ In a medium saucepan over medium-high heat, combine the water, milk, butter, sugar, and salt and cook, stirring occasionally, until the mixture comes to a rapid simmer, 5 to 8 minutes. Remove from the heat, then add the flour and stir vigorously with a rubber spatula or wooden spoon to form a dough. Decrease the heat to medium and cook, stirring constantly, until there is a thin film at the bottom of the saucepan, about 3 minutes.

☞ Transfer the dough to a large bowl and cool for 10 minutes, stirring occasionally to help release some of the heat. Crack the eggs into a liquid measuring cup. After 10 minutes, beat in one egg with an electric hand mixer at medium speed and continue beating until fully combined. Beat in the remaining four eggs, one at a time, to make a smooth and glossy dough, stopping to scrape down the sides of the bowl occasionally.

☞ Transfer half of the dough to a pastry bag or large plastic storage bag fitted with a ½-inch / 1.3cm round tip. Pipe a small amount of dough in the four corners of the baking sheet and stick the dough to the parchment paper; this will ensure that the parchment paper doesn't lift up while you pipe the rest of the dough and during baking. Working in an up and down motion (do not swirl), pipe about thirty small mounds of dough onto the baking sheet, about 1¼ inches / 3cm wide and 1 inch / 2.5cm tall, and spacing them about 1 inch / 2.5cm apart. Lightly wet one of your fingers, then lightly press down on any pointed tops on the puffs. Fill the pastry bag with the remaining dough and repeat with the second prepared baking sheet, making about sixty puffs total.

☛ Place both baking sheets into the oven and bake for 15 minutes. Immediately decrease the oven temperature to 375°F / 190°C. Continue to bake until the puffs are deep golden brown, crisp, and sound hollow, 15 to 20 additional minutes (30 to 35 minutes total baking time). Remove from the oven and use the tip of a sharp paring knife to cut a small slit on the side of each puff to release any steam that is trapped inside and keep the puffs crispy. Return to the oven, turn off the heat, crack the door open 2 inches / 5cm, and cool in the oven for 30 minutes. Transfer the baked puffs to a wire rack and cool completely.

☛ **FOR THE MACERATED STRAWBERRIES:** In a medium bowl, combine the strawberries, Champagne, and sugar. Set aside, stirring occasionally, until the sugar dissolves and the berries are juicy, about 15 minutes.

☛ **FOR THE PINK STRAWBERRY SUGAR:** Place a fine-mesh strainer over a small bowl, spoon the confectioners' sugar into the strainer, and push through into the bowl. Set aside. In a spice grinder, process the freeze-dried strawberries into a fine powder. Transfer to the fine-mesh strainer and use the back of a spoon or rubber spatula to push the ground berries through the strainer and into the bowl (discard any seeds). Whisk to combine with the confectioners' sugar and set aside.

☛ **TO ASSEMBLE:** Use a serrated knife to cut each cooled cream puff in half, pipe some of the filling onto the puff bottom (it should extend slightly beyond the pastry), use a fork to lift some strawberry slices out of the Champagne syrup and place on top of the cream, then put the puff top back on. Repeat this until all of the puffs are filled, then dust the tops with the strawberry sugar.

☛ Transfer onto serving platters or arrange onto a dessert tower and serve immediately.

PEACH AND BOURBON SMASH

"THERE ARE NO GEMSTONE MINES IN GEORGIA."
—COLIN BRIDGERTON TO PENELOPE FEATHERINGTON

Makes 1 serving

5 mint leaves, plus 1 sprig for garnish
3 peach slices
½ lemon, cut into quarters
1 ounce / 30ml orange liqueur, such as Cointreau or triple sec
¼ ounce / 7ml simple syrup (page 62, optional, if you prefer a slightly sweeter cocktail)
2 ounces / 60ml bourbon
Ice cubes, as needed

The new Lord Featherington may have revealed himself to be a charlatan—his "American rubies" were nothing but a convincing counterfeit, as anyone who has traveled to the former colonies could have told you. But he did encounter two true treasures in his travels: Kentucky bourbon and Georgia peaches, a match made in culinary heaven. This refreshing smash-style cocktail takes the sting out of being swindled by the ersatz lord.

Combine the mint leaves, two of the peach slices, the lemon quarters, the orange liqueur, and the simple syrup (if using) in a cocktail shaker. Muddle the ingredients, then add the bourbon and fill the shaker with ice. Shake until chilled and strain into an old-fashioned glass filled with ice. Cut the remaining peach slice and affix to the rim of the glass. Garnish with the mint sprig and serve.

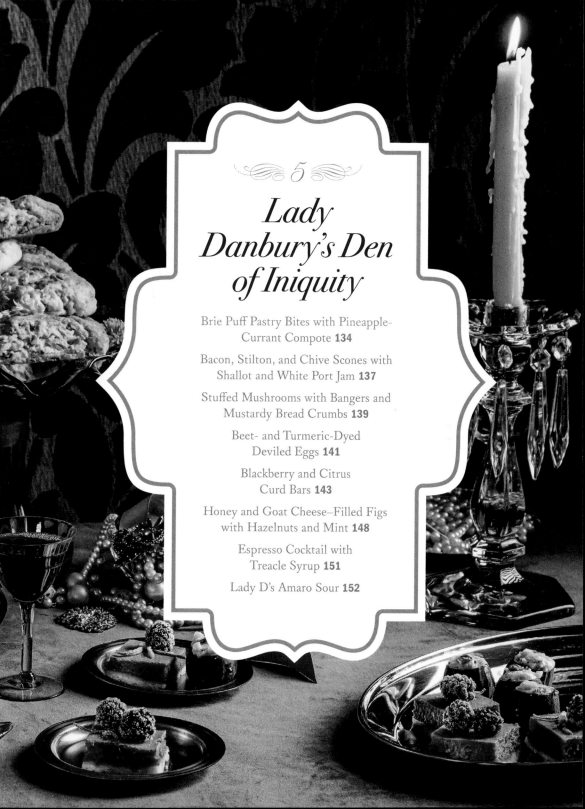

5

Lady Danbury's Den of Iniquity

"Seeing how you entertain yourself, I rather think you the victor, Lady Danbury."
—Daphne Bridgerton

The gentlemen of the ton love to sneak away to their clubs, where they smugly assume they have a monopoly on tobacco, fine spirits, and games of chance. Little do they know, married and widowed women have a special soirée of their own. Behind the weighty doors of Lady Danbury's salon, the prim and proper grandes dames of London society engage in all sorts of louche behavior. They smoke, drink, gamble, and gossip with impunity. Or, as Lady Trowbridge so artfully put it to Daphne on the latter's inaugural visit: "First, a woman takes her wedding vows, then we gamblers take her virtue."

When planning your own "den of iniquity," it is up to you to decide what sort of libertine behavior you wish to engage in. Perhaps you'll forbid the stiff, buttoned-up formality of workwear and insist your guests don their softest attire: silk, velvet, velour, and feathers are highly encouraged. Perhaps you'll strew your plumpest pillows and blankets on the floor so that guests can slouchily enjoy their refreshments. But, please, do not limit your soirée to the espoused. All people, married or not, deserve one evening when they get to throw responsibility and respectability to the wind.

Game Night

Do you like a wager, big or small? Would you rather play a good game than spend hours in small talk? This is your event. Host a stylish evening of gaming, inspired by the inimitable Lady Danbury. Invite people who like to compete (you know who they are), offer several gaming options (you never know which will be the evening's hit), and prepare delicious food and drink to keep your company at the tables.

DÉCOR

This is not the night for pale pastels or debutante white. If an overeager guest spills red wine reaching for a playing card or leaping up to celebrate a win, your nice linens should not suffer the consequences. Consider fresh green felt or dark velvet for table coverings. The ambience should be dark and moody, with desk lamps or LED lanterns at each gaming station to spotlight the proceedings. Lay out stylish card decks, poker chips, and multiple sets of instructions for each game you feature. On the side, set up a vintage chessboard, backgammon set, and dice cups to encourage one-on-one games. The centerpiece will be a banquet of food with plenty of jewel-toned candles, a bouquet of crimson roses and black dahlias, and bowls heaped with luscious persimmons and grapes.

FOOD + DRINK

Your guests will have cards in one hand and a snack or drink in the other—so take the phrase "finger foods" quite literally. Save the salad for another day and make handheld, visually striking snacks like Beet- and Turmeric-Dyed Deviled Eggs (page 141), Honey and Goat Cheese–Filled Figs (page 148), and Stuffed Mushrooms with Bangers and Mustardy Bread Crumbs (page 139). Paired with a bulk batch of espresso martinis, these hearty appetizers will keep your guests fueled for a long night of fun.

Wagering was a popular pastime among the upper crust of Regency England—and unfortunately, it was not unheard of for a gentleman to gamble away an entire family fortune at his club. If you set a low price for chips (25 cents, 50 cents, or a dollar), your guests can gamble the night away without fear of losing the ancestral pile.

BRIE PUFF PASTRY BITES

with Pineapple-Currant Compote

Makes 12 pieces

¼ cup / 30g dried currants
2 tablespoons gold rum
12 ounces / 340g finely
   chopped ripe pineapple
   (about 2 cups)
1 tablespoon black treacle (see
   Cook's Note, page 151)
Pinch of kosher salt
4 ounces / 115g Brie, cold
Unsalted butter, for greasing
All-purpose flour, for dusting
1 sheet frozen puff pastry
   dough, defrosted according to
   package directions
1 egg

No fruit has captured the imagination of the ton quite like the pineapple. In Mayfair, showcasing "King Pine" on your dining table is an immediate signal to your guests that you are a person with money and access. The wealthiest aficionados have even installed pineries—hothouses dedicated specifically to the cultivation of pineapples—on their country estates.

Sourcing pineapples is no trouble at all for Lady Danbury, and with this delicious cheese, pineapple, and pastry bite, she subtly announces to her guests that no ingredient is too precious for her stately table.

☞ In a small bowl, combine the currants and rum and set aside at room temperature for 30 minutes.

☞ In a medium saucepan over medium heat, combine the chopped pineapple, treacle, a pinch of salt, and a large splash of water. Stir to combine and bring the mixture to a rapid simmer, about 5 minutes, stirring occasionally. Continue to cook, adjusting the heat as needed to maintain a simmer, until the pineapple is tender, about 10 minutes. Spoon out a little more than half of the pineapple into a medium bowl and set aside. Add the rum-soaked currants to the pineapple remaining in the saucepan and continue to simmer until the sauce has reduced to almost dry, about 10 additional minutes. Pour into the bowl with the reserved pineapple, stir to combine, and set aside to cool completely. The pineapple and currant compote will thicken as it cools.

☞ Cut the Brie into twelve ½ by 1-inch / 1.3 by 2.5cm squares. If you have any leftover cheese after cutting the twelve squares, cut the extra cheese into twelve equal pieces. Transfer all of the cheese to a large plate and chill in the refrigerator until you are ready to assemble.

☞ Generously butter a 12-cup muffin pan and set aside.

☞ Lightly dust a work surface with flour and roll the puff pastry into a 10-inch / 25cm square. Cut the square into three equal strips following the natural seams on the pastry. Turn each strip so that the longer side is facing you and cut crosswise into four equal pieces (twelve pieces total). Crack the egg into a small bowl, add a splash of water, and beat until well combined and smooth. Set the egg wash aside.

☞ Place a pastry square in the center of each muffin cup and use your fingers to lightly press the pastry onto the bottom and partially up the sides of the cups. Put one square of Brie into each muffin cup, then divvy up any extra cheese into the cups as well. Top the cheese evenly with spoonfuls of the cooled pineapple and currant compote (leave behind any extra juice). Brush the inside corners of the puff pastry with some of the egg wash. Bring the four edges of each puff pastry square together toward the center, overlapping them slightly so that the pastry adheres but parts of the filling are still exposed. Chill the puff pastry bites in the refrigerator for 20 minutes while you preheat the oven.

☞ Preheat the oven to 400°F / 200°C.

☞ Brush the puff pastry with more egg wash and bake for 20 minutes. Rotate the muffin pan and reduce the oven temperature to 350°F / 175°C. Continue to bake until the puff pastry is deeply golden brown and cooked through, 5 to 10 additional minutes.

☞ Take the muffin pan out of the oven and place on a wire rack to cool for 5 minutes. Run a small confectioners' spatula or butter knife around the edges of each puff pastry bite, remove from the pan, and place on a platter. Serve immediately while the bites are nice and warm.

BACON, STILTON, AND CHIVE SCONES

with Shallot and White Port Jam

Makes
24 scones

8 slices bacon

3 cups / 420g all-purpose flour, plus additional for dusting

1½ tablespoons baking powder

2 tablespoons sugar

2½ teaspoons kosher salt

6 tablespoons / 85g cold unsalted butter, cut into small cubes

3 ounces / 85g Stilton cheese, crumbled into large pieces

½ cup / 23g thinly sliced chives

1⅔ cups / 395ml heavy cream, cold, plus additional for brushing

Shallot and White Port Jam (recipe follows; also see Cook's Note)

These petite scones are a perfect treat for any lover of fine English cheese. Etiquette dictates that a scone should always be torn in half, rather than sliced; cutting a scone with a knife is deleterious to its texture, which may become claggy and dense.

Cook's Note: If you'd rather not make homemade jam, serve the scones with store-bought onion jam or fig preserves.

☞ Preheat the oven to 375°F / 190°C. Line one rimmed baking sheet with aluminum foil and one baking sheet with parchment paper. Line a large plate with a couple of layers of paper towels and set aside.

☞ Arrange the bacon in a single layer on the foil-lined baking sheet and bake in the oven until the bacon is browned and crispy, about 25 minutes. Transfer the cooked bacon to the prepared plate and cool completely. Turn off the oven.

☞ In a large bowl, whisk together the flour, baking powder, sugar, and salt. Coarsely chop the cooled bacon and set aside.

☞ Add the butter to the flour mixture and use your fingers to break up the butter and work it into the flour until the mixture is crumbly. Add the cheese, chives, and bacon and use your hands to stir until they are coated in the flour mixture. Drizzle one-third of the chilled heavy cream over the dry ingredients, then gently toss and stir with your hands. Repeat this two additional times until all of the heavy cream has been added and the mixture has come together to form a shaggy dough (a few dry patches in the dough is fine).

☞ Lightly dust a work surface with flour. Divide the dough into two large mounds. Use your hands to pat each portion of dough into a ¾-inch / 2cm thick disk that is about 6 inches / 15cm around. Use a large knife or bench scraper to cut each disk into twelve equal wedges (twenty-four scones total). Transfer

Recipe continues

to the parchment paper–lined baking sheet, spacing the scones evenly apart.

☞ Chill the formed scones in the refrigerator for 20 minutes while you preheat the oven to 425°F / 220°C.

☞ Brush the top of the scones with additional heavy cream and bake until the scones are puffed and golden brown, about 20 minutes, rotating the baking sheet once after 10 minutes. Remove them from the oven and cool the scones on the baking sheet for 10 minutes. Transfer to a platter and serve warm alongside the jam.

MR. FINCH:
Oh! What a delectable frock! Almost the exact shade of the double Gloucester your mother served at tea this afternoon. I so love cheese.

PHILIPPA FEATHERINGTON:
As do I, Mr. Finch! Though, I must say, I do prefer a Stilton to a cheddar.

SHALLOT AND WHITE PORT JAM
Makes about 2 scant cups / 170g

1½ tablespoons unsalted butter
1½ tablespoons vegetable oil
2 pounds / 900g large shallots (14 to 16 total), thinly sliced
Kosher salt and freshly ground black pepper
¾ cup / 175ml white port wine
¼ cup / 60ml white wine vinegar
¼ cup / 50g packed dark brown sugar
1½ teaspoons finely chopped fresh thyme leaves
Water (optional)

☞ In a large Dutch oven or heavy pot set over medium to medium-high heat, combine the butter and vegetable oil and cook until the butter melts and starts to foam. Add the shallots, season with salt and pepper, and cook, stirring occasionally until the shallots are tender, browned in spots, and starting to stick to the bottom of the Dutch oven, about 20 minutes.

☞ Add the port, 3 tablespoons of the white wine vinegar, and 3 tablespoons of the brown sugar. Use a wooden spoon to scrape up any browned bits at the bottom of the Dutch oven. Decrease the heat to medium, stir in the thyme and continue to cook, stirring occasionally, until the shallots are golden brown, caramelized, and jammy, about 1 additional hour. If the shallots start to appear dry at any point and stick to the bottom of the pot, stir in a splash of water. Once the shallots are caramelized, stir in the remaining 1 tablespoon of vinegar, 1 tablespoon of brown sugar, and a large splash of water and cook until the sugar is melted into the shallots. Season with salt and pepper, then transfer to a bowl. Serve warm or at room temperature.

☞ Transfer any leftover jam into an airtight container and store in the refrigerator for up to 7 days.

STUFFED MUSHROOMS

with Bangers and Mustardy Bread Crumbs

Makes 16 pieces

16 large cremini mushrooms
(about 1 pound / 450g),
stems removed and reserved
2 tablespoons vegetable oil
Kosher salt and freshly ground
black pepper
4 ounces / 115g cooked British-
style bangers (see Cook's
Note), casing removed; very
finely chopped
1 small shallot, finely chopped
Half of a small red bell pepper,
finely chopped
2 tablespoons heavy cream
¼ cup / 15g plus ⅓ cup /
20g panko bread crumbs
2 ounces / 57 grams Red
Leicester, Cheshire, or aged
cheddar cheese, crumbled
2 tablespoons chopped fresh
flat-leaf parsley
1 tablespoon unsalted butter
1 garlic clove, finely grated
¼ teaspoon smoked paprika
¼ teaspoon dry mustard powder

You might hear the term "finger foods" and think of dainty little canapés that look lovely in hand but do nothing to fill one's
stomach. There's nothing precious or dainty about these hearty
mushroom bites that are brimming with flavor and fillings:
smoky English sausage, pungent cheese, and garlicky bread
crumbs with an assertive mustard and paprika kick.

*Cook's Note: You can substitute any cooked mild pork sausage for the
British-style bangers.*

☞ Preheat the oven to 400°F / 200°C.

☞ Finely chop the mushroom stems and set aside. Place the
mushroom caps hollow side up on a baking sheet and brush all
over with 1 tablespoon of the vegetable oil. Bake until the mushrooms are just tender, about 10 minutes. Remove from the oven
and discard any liquid that has accumulated in the caps. Season
the hot mushrooms lightly with salt and pepper and set aside.

☞ In a large skillet over medium-high heat, warm the remaining 1 tablespoon of oil. Add the bangers and mushroom stems and
cook, stirring occasionally, until the sausage is browned in spots
and the mushrooms are tender, 6 to 8 minutes. Add the shallot and
bell pepper, season with salt and pepper, and cook, stirring occasionally, until the vegetables are tender, 6 to 8 minutes. Transfer
to a mixing bowl and stir in the heavy cream, ¼ cup / 15g of the
panko bread crumbs, the crumbled cheese, and 1 tablespoon of the
parsley. Taste and season with additional salt and pepper.

☞ Spoon the filling into the roasted mushroom caps, lightly
packing the filling. Bake until lightly browned and the cheese is
melted, 17 to 20 minutes.

☞ Meanwhile, in a medium skillet over medium heat, melt the
butter. Add the garlic and cook, stirring constantly, for 30 seconds. Add the remaining ⅓ cup / 20g of panko bread crumbs, the
smoked paprika, mustard powder, a large pinch of salt, and several grinds of pepper. Toast the bread crumbs, stirring frequently,
until lightly browned, 6 to 8 minutes. Pour the bread crumbs into
a small bowl and stir in the remaining 1 tablespoon of parsley.

☞ Remove the stuffed mushrooms from the oven and sprinkle
with the toasted bread crumbs. Transfer to a platter and serve.

BEET- AND TURMERIC-
DYED DEVILED EGGS

Makes
24 pieces

6 ounces / 170g red beets
    (about 1 large or 2 small),
    scrubbed
4 cups / 950ml water
1 cup / 240ml distilled white
    vinegar
3 tablespoons sugar
2 bay leaves
Kosher salt
1 tablespoon ground turmeric
12 eggs (see Cook's Note)
½ cup / 120g mayonnaise
2 tablespoons whole-grain
    mustard
Freshly ground pepper
1 tablespoon coarsely chopped
    fresh chervil leaves, plus
    whole leaves for garnish

It is no coincidence that these beet-dyed deviled eggs perfectly match the rich red and purple attire Lady Danbury so often wears. With her wardrobe, Lady Danbury underscores her strength and power every time she steps into a room. The vibrant hue of the beet-dyed eggs is similarly designed to shock, awe—and, ultimately, delight. Although she does not wear yellow herself (she'll leave that to the poor Miss Penelope Featherington), Lady Danbury nevertheless loves the golden turmeric-dyed eggs as well.

Cook's Note: Older eggs tend to be easier to peel; so, if possible, try to use eggs that have been in your refrigerator for at least a week (even longer is preferable). As eggs age, both the inner and outer membranes stick less to the white albumen, which make the shells easier to peel.

☞ Place a box grater in a medium saucepan and grate the beets on the largest hole of the grater directly into the saucepan (this will contain the beet juices). Add 2 cups / 475ml of the water, ½ cup / 120ml of the white vinegar, 1½ tablespoons of the sugar, 1 bay leaf, and 1 teaspoon salt. Turn the heat to medium-high and bring to a boil, about 10 minutes. Reduce the heat to a simmer and cook, stirring occasionally, until the grated beets are tender but not falling apart and the pickling liquid is a deep reddish-purple hue, about 10 additional minutes. Strain into a medium bowl or a large heatproof jar, press down on the grated beets to extract as much liquid as possible, and cool the beet pickling liquid completely.

☞ In a clean saucepan, combine the turmeric and the remaining 2 cups / 475ml of water, remaining ½ cup / 120ml of white vinegar, 1½ tablespoons of sugar, 1 bay leaf, and 1 teaspoon salt. Turn the heat to medium and bring to a simmer, stirring occasionally, about 10 minutes. Continue to simmer for 10 additional minutes, then pour the turmeric pickling liquid into a second medium bowl or large heatproof jar and cool completely.

Recipe continues

☞ Meanwhile, bring a large pot filled halfway with water to a boil. Use a slotted spoon to gently lower the eggs into the water. Reduce the heat slightly so that the water is at a rapid simmer but not vigorously boiling and cook for 12 minutes. Fill a large bowl with ice water. After 12 minutes, turn off the heat and use a slotted spoon to transfer the eggs to the ice bath. Cool for 10 minutes, then peel the eggs. Transfer six eggs to the cooled beet pickling liquid and the other six to the turmeric pickling liquid. Cover the bowls or jars and refrigerate for at least 6 hours and up to 24 hours. The longer the eggs sit in the pickling liquid, the more vibrant their color will be.

☞ Use a slotted spoon to remove the eggs from pickling liquids and pat the eggs dry. Be careful not to let the two types of eggs touch each other because the beet color will stain the turmeric eggs. Halve the eggs lengthwise and carefully transfer the yolks to a medium bowl. Use a fork to mash the yolks until they are as smooth as possible. Add the mayonnaise, mustard, and several large grinds of black pepper and use a rubber spatula to stir together. Use the back of the spatula to further break down any pieces of egg yolk. The mixture should be very smooth except for the grains of mustard. Stir in the chopped chervil, then season with salt. Fit a large open star piping tip into a disposable pastry bag or large resealable plastic storage bag with a corner snipped off and transfer the filling into the bag.

☞ Place the dyed egg white halves on a platter. Pipe the yolk filling evenly into the egg whites, garnish with chervil leaves, and serve.

BLACKBERRY AND CITRUS CURD BARS

Makes 16 bars

SHORTBREAD CRUST

½ cup / 110g (1 stick) cold
  unsalted butter, cut into small
  cubes, plus additional for
  greasing
¾ cup / 105g plus 1 tablespoon
  all-purpose flour
¼ cup / 30g confectioners'
  sugar
2 tablespoons cornstarch
½ teaspoon kosher salt

BLACKBERRY AND
CITRUS CURD

8 ounces / 225g blackberries
  (about 2 cups)
¼ cup / 60ml fresh tangerine
  juice
½ cup / 100g granulated sugar
¼ cup / 60ml fresh lemon juice
1 tablespoon cornstarch
¼ teaspoon kosher salt
2 eggs plus 2 egg yolks, at room
  temperature
4 tablespoons / 55g cold
  unsalted butter, cubed
3 tablespoons / 60g seedless
  blackberry preserves

SUGARED BLACKBERRIES
AND ROSEMARY

⅓ cup / 80ml water
⅓ cup / 65g plus
  3 tablespoons sugar
Small pinch of kosher salt
8 (1-inch / 2.5cm) rosemary
  sprigs
8 small blackberries

You may ask, "Another purple offering from Lady Danbury?" To which this author must reply, *Are you really surprised?* Lady Danbury is rather famous for knowing what she likes—and offering no apologies for it. Here is a luscious citrus curd bar in her signature shade, with a minimal but oh-so-elegant garnish of candied blackberries and rosemary sprigs.

Cook's Note: These bars can be baked and chilled for up to 5 days, but do not add the sugared blackberries or rosemary until ready to serve.

☞ **FOR THE SHORTBREAD CRUST:** Lightly grease an 8-inch / 20cm square baking pan with butter. Line the pan with two overlapping pieces of parchment paper, leaving an overhang of about 2 inches / 5cm on all sides. Set aside.

☞ Combine the flour, confectioners' sugar, cornstarch, and salt in the bowl of a food processor. Pulse several times to combine. Add the butter and pulse until the mixture looks like finely grated Parmesan cheese. Press the dough evenly into the bottom of the prepared baking pan. Chill in the refrigerator while you preheat the oven.

☞ Preheat the oven to 350°F / 175°C.

☞ Bake until the dough is lightly golden brown and set, about 25 minutes, rotating the baking pan once after 15 minutes.

☞ Remove the crust from the oven and use a fork to prick the crust all over, but only going about ¼ inch / 6mm deep. Cool completely on a wire rack. Reduce the oven temperature to 325°F / 165°C.

☞ **FOR THE BLACKBERRY AND CITRUS CURD:** In a large saucepan over medium heat, combine the blackberries and 2 tablespoons of the tangerine juice and bring to a simmer, 3 to 5 minutes. Simmer until most of the blackberries have broken down, about 5 additional minutes, stirring occasionally and smashing some of the berries against the side of the saucepan.

Recipe continues

☞ Strain the blackberry mixture through a fine-mesh strainer into a large bowl, pressing down on the berries to get every bit of juice out. Rinse out the strainer, place over a medium bowl, and set aside (you will use this later to strain the finished curd). Wash out the saucepan and fill it with 1 inch / 2.5cm of water. Bring the water to a boil over medium-high heat, then lower the heat to maintain an active simmer.

☞ To the bowl with the strained blackberry mixture, add the granulated sugar, the remaining 2 tablespoons of tangerine juice, the lemon juice, cornstarch, and salt and whisk until well combined and smooth. Add the eggs and egg yolks and whisk again until smooth. Place the bowl on top of the saucepan of simmering water and cook, whisking constantly, until the mixture thickens to a consistency similar to a milkshake, about 15 minutes. Remove the bowl from the heat and slowly whisk in the butter, a couple of cubes at a time, whisking well after each addition. Once all of the butter has been incorporated, whisk in the blackberry preserves until smooth.

☞ Strain the curd through the reserved fine-mesh strainer into the medium bowl. Give the curd a good stir, then pour it on top of the cooled shortbread crust, spreading it out into an even layer. Return the baking pan to the oven and bake until the curd is slightly puffed and set around the edges but still ever so slightly wobbly in the center, 20 to 25 minutes, rotating the baking pan once after 10 minutes.

☞ Cool on a wire rack at room temperature for 1 hour, then transfer to the refrigerator to cool completely, at least 2 hours and up to overnight.

☞ **FOR THE SUGARED BLACKBERRIES AND ROSEMARY:** In a small saucepan over medium heat, combine the water, ⅓ cup / 65g of the sugar, and salt, and warm, stirring frequently, until the sugar completely dissolves, about 2 minutes. Pour this syrup into a small bowl or mug and cool completely, about 10 minutes. Line a small baking sheet or large plate with parchment paper and set aside.

☞ Add the rosemary sprigs to the syrup and let sit for 5 minutes. Use small tongs or chopsticks to remove the rosemary from the syrup (allow any excess syrup to drip away) and transfer to the prepared baking sheet or plate in a single layer. Repeat the process with the blackberries. Allow to dry at room temperature for 1 hour. Put the remaining 3 tablespoons of sugar in a small bowl. One by one, pick up each rosemary sprig and flick off any remaining syrup back onto the baking sheet or plate, then quickly roll in the sugar. Place the rosemary onto a new dry plate. Repeat with the blackberries and transfer to the same plate as the rosemary.

☞ To serve, use the parchment paper to lift the blackberry and citrus curd crust out of the baking pan and place on a cutting board. Use a serrated knife to cut into sixteen even squares. Transfer the bars to a platter and top each with either a sugared blackberry or rosemary sprig. Serve immediately.

Games of Chance

LADY TROWBRIDGE:

The earl would have my head if he knew how much money I have lost.

KITTY LANGHAM:

The earl is but two years old.

LADY TROWBRIDGE:

Hmm. Well, then, I'm in luck, am I not?

Most members of the ton have more money than they know what to do with. As such, they've found a way to place stakes on just about everything: horse racing, cards, human fights, rooster fights, even silly feats of daring (who can jump the farthest or down a pint fastest). But you don't have to be obscenely wealthy to enjoy a little gambling here and there. Set a modest cap on wagers—or consider playing with quarters, to ensure none of your guests wind up in hock by night's end. Any of the games below are a fine way to spice up an evening.

Whist

This is the precursor of modern-day bridge, and it is far and away the most popular card game of the Regency era. Four players play in pairs. Starting with the player on her left, the dealer deals out all fifty-two cards (thirteen to each player), face down. The last card dealt is the trump card, which is left face up on the table. (For our purposes, imagine it is the queen of hearts.) All other cards of the same suit (in our hypothetical game, hearts) are considered trumps for the rest of the hand.

The player on the dealer's left plays the first card. The player may play any card at all in hand. When the dealer plays to the first trick, they pick up the trump card and it becomes part of the dealer's hand. Play continues clockwise, with each player laying down a card of the same suit. You *must* follow suit if you can. Whoever plays the highest card (aces are high) wins the trick. If you cannot play the suit, you can play any card. If you play a trump card, you win the trick. In our imaginary game, the first player plays a king of diamonds. The second player plays a three of diamonds, and the third player plays six of diamonds. The fourth player has no diamonds at all, so this player plays a two of hearts. Since hearts are trumps, the fourth player takes the trick.

The winner of each trick leads next and can play any card in hand.

At the end of each round, i.e., after all the cards have been played, count the number of tricks each two-player team has won. Each trick won after six counts as one point. (For example, if team A won eight tricks, they get two points; team B, with five tricks, gets zero points.) Whichever team gets to ten points first wins.

Vingt-et-un

Blackjack enthusiasts will enjoy vingt-et-un, a particularly wonderful game for a crowd, as any number of players can participate. The dealer passes each player a card, face down, at which point all the players except the dealer look at their own card and declare their stakes (1, 2, 3, or more tokens or chips). When every player has staked, the dealer looks at her dealt card and may choose to double all the stakes (or not). The dealer deals everyone another card, face down. If at this point anyone has a ten and an ace (totaling twenty-one), they declare a "natural." Every player, including the dealer, must pay them double their declared stake, unless someone else has a natural (in which case the two naturals draw).

Play continues with the dealer asking each of the players if they want to "stand" or choose another card. A player may continue to ask for more cards until the cards reach or exceed twenty-one ("bust") or the player decides to stand. If a player goes bust, the player must pay the stake to the dealer. The dealer can also draw cards; and if the dealer reaches vingt-et-un, the dealer receives double stakes from everyone who stands with less than twenty-one. When any opponent has twenty-one, but the dealer does not, the dealer pays double stakes. If no one has twenty-one, the dealer pays a single stake to those whose scores are higher, and the dealer receives a single stake from those whose score is lower. Any player with the same score as the dealer "draws." If the dealer exceeds twenty-one, the dealer pays everyone who has not thrown up their cards.

Luminaries

Modern readers may know this game as Celebrity. But for a *Bridgerton*-appropriate twist on the classic, instruct your guests to write down the names of in-world characters (members of the ton, tradespeople, opera singers, servants) or notable public figures from the era (the Duke of Wellington, Lord Byron, and the like).

Divide your group into two even teams. Everyone should write the name of five luminaries on five cards. Fold all the cards in half and place them in a hat or bowl. The first player from team A selects a card from the hat. Start a timer for 60 seconds. The first player can give whatever clue might lead the team to identify their luminary—but without saying any part of the name or a nickname. Every time one of the teammates guesses correctly, the team gets a point. The first player picks another card and gives more clues until 60 seconds have expired.

At this point, the first player of team B selects a card and starts the timer. Their team repeats the process, guessing as many luminaries as possible in 60 seconds. Tally the points at the end of each round. Whichever team has the most points after five rounds wins.

HONEY AND GOAT CHEESE–FILLED FIGS
with Hazelnuts and Mint

Makes 16 to 20 pieces

1 pound / 453g small ripe fresh figs (16 to 20 total depending on size)

1 tablespoon honey, plus additional for drizzling

⅓ cup / 85g creamy goat cheese (chèvre), at room temperature

Kosher salt and freshly ground black pepper

6 large fresh mint leaves

2 tablespoons coarsely chopped, dry-roasted unsalted hazelnuts

There is a reason the Romans considered figs to be a gift from Bacchus, the god of wine and carnal delights. A single bite of these perfectly ripe morsels, bursting with flavor and a creamy goat cheese filling, is enough to make a debutante blush. But we are not blushing debutantes here in this den of iniquity; we are boisterous ladies who know how to appreciate a beautiful (if voluptuous) hors d'oeuvre.

☞ Cut off the top ¼ inch / 6mm of each fig and use the back of a small spoon to scoop out some of the seeds from each fig (about ½ teaspoon each). You are essentially creating small fig "cups." Transfer the seeds to a small bowl, add the honey, and use a fork to smash the seeds and honey until the mixture is smooth and jammy. Add the goat cheese, a pinch of salt, and several large grinds of black pepper, then stir until well combined and smooth.

☞ Coarsely chop four of the mint leaves and fold into the goat cheese mixture. Transfer the filling into a small piping bag or plastic storage bag and cut a small opening on one corner of the bag that is a little larger than ¼ inch / 6mm. Pipe the filling into each fig so that the filling comes slightly out of the top. Transfer the stuffed figs to a serving platter, drizzle with additional honey, and sprinkle with the chopped hazelnuts. Coarsely chop the remaining two mint leaves, sprinkle over the stuffed figs along with a couple grinds of additional black pepper, and serve.

ESPRESSO COCKTAIL
with Treacle Syrup

Makes 1 serving

1½ ounces / 44ml vodka
1 ounce / 30ml coffee liqueur,
   such as Kahlúa
1 ounce / 30ml freshly brewed
   espresso, cooled
1 to 2 tablespoons / 16.5 to
   33g Brown Sugar and
   Treacle Syrup (depending on
   sweetness preference) (recipe
   below)
3 dark chocolate–covered coffee
   beans for garnish

Coffee in the evening? It may seem shocking, but when it is eleven o'clock at night, you are winning at whist, and you are unwilling to leave the company of your dearest friends, sometimes drastic measures are required. This espresso cocktail is just the thing to keep you pert and alert for as long as you decide to stay out on the town.

Cook's Note: The bittersweet and slightly fruity treacle syrup is fantastic stirred into a cup of hot or iced coffee. If you have trouble sourcing black treacle, you can use an equal parts mixture of blackstrap molasses and honey instead.

☛ To a cocktail shaker filled with ice, add the vodka, coffee liqueur, espresso, and brown sugar and treacle syrup. Place the lid on the cocktail shaker and vigorously shake until the mixture is very cold and foamy, 30 seconds to 1 minute. Strain into a martini glass, garnish with the chocolate-covered coffee beans, and serve immediately.

BROWN SUGAR AND TREACLE SYRUP
Makes about 1¼ cups / 330g

½ cup / 100g packed light brown sugar
¼ cup / 95g black treacle
   (see Cook's Note)
¾ cup / 175ml water

☛ In a small saucepan over medium-low heat, stir together the brown sugar, black treacle, and water. Cook, stirring occasionally, until the sugar and treacle melt together and the mixture is hot and steamy, about 5 minutes. Remove from the heat and cool completely at room temperature.

☛ Transfer the syrup into a glass jar. Use immediately or store in the refrigerator for up to 14 days.

LADY D'S AMARO SOUR

"I SHALL NEED SOMEONE ELSE TO SEEK ME
A GLASS OF THE RATAFIA." —LADY DANBURY

Makes 1 serving

1½ ounces / 44ml amaro
¾ ounce / 22ml bourbon
1 ounce / 30ml freshly
   squeezed lemon juice
¼ ounce / 7ml simple syrup
   (page 62)
1 egg white
Ice
Lemon peel and cocktail cherry
   for garnish

Ratafia is a style of cordial made in parts of France, Spain, and Italy. It is essentially brandy infused with nuts, fruits, herbs, and spices—often cherry, peach, or apricot kernels or the essence of bitter almonds. Modern readers may struggle to find ratafia; however, amaro (a style of bittersweet Italian liqueur) is widely available at most well-stocked liquor stores and is an interesting substitute. Amari range in flavor from pleasantly bracing to assertively bitter, so if you're new to the stuff, ask the clerk to point you in the direction of a "gateway amaro," such as Averna or Lucano.

☞ Combine the amaro, bourbon, lemon juice, simple syrup, and egg white in a cocktail shaker without ice and shake for 10 seconds to incorporate the egg white. Add ice to the shaker and continue shaking until chilled. Strain into an old-fashioned glass filled with ice. Garnish with the lemon peel and cocktail cherry and serve.

Resources

British Specialty Ingredients

For mustards, kippers, bangers, and more:

Kitty O'Shea's Irish & UK Market
4692 Eagle Rock Boulevard
Eagle Rock, CA 90041
kittyosheasmarket.com

Myers of Keswick
634 Hudson Street
New York, NY 10014
myersofkeswick.com

Tea Suppliers

Rare Tea Co
rareteacompany.us

Flowerhead Tea
flowerheadtea.com

Té Company Tea
163 West 10th Street
New York, NY 10014
tecompanytea.com

For official Bridgerton teas:

The Republic of Tea
republicoftea.com

Spice Purveyors

Oaktown Spice Shop
546 Grand Avenue
Oakland, CA 94610
oaktownspiceshop.com

Kalustyan's
123 Lexington Avenue
New York, NY 10016
foodsofnations.com

For single-origin turmeric, cloves, and cardamom:

Diaspora Co.
diasporaco.com

Indian Markets

For dried flowers, spices, teas, and more:

India Sweets & Spices (two locations)
3126 Los Feliz Boulevard
Los Angeles, CA 90039

567 South Fairfax Avenue
Los Angeles, CA 90036

indiashop.us

Servingware and Kitchenware

Williams-Sonoma
williams-sonoma.com

For antique butter molds, copper gelatin molds, and tiered serving stands:

Etsy
etsy.com

Cookin': Recycled Gourmet Appurtenances
339 Divisadero Street
San Francisco, CA 94117

Acknowledgments

FIRST AND BIGGEST THANKS GO TO SUSAN VU, WHO IS NOT ONLY A CULI-nary genius but also a kind, hilarious, too-good-to-be-real person. We are so lucky that you blessed this book with your many talents. Thank you for always writing perfect recipes, and for always knowing when I needed a saucy *Bridgerton*-inspired GIF to keep me motivated.

Thanks also to Sarah Malarkey, Lydia Estrada, Ian Dingman, Mark McCauslin, Patricia Shaw, Jessica Heim, and the entire team at Random House Worlds for being such excellent publishing partners. Thank you to Sandie Bailey, Shuhui Wen, Leslie Bray, Catherine Yan Lustro, Jennifer Joel, and the team at Shondaland for creating the world of *Bridgerton* and inviting us to join the party. Thank you to Brad Thomas Parsons, my cocktail consigliere and author of the indispensable book *Amaro*, for providing information and inspiration for the Amaro Sour on page 152. Thank you to Rica Allanic at the David Black Agency for being the best literary agent in the business.

And as always, thank you to my mom, MaryGael Timberlake. When she heard I was working on this project, she snapped into action, reading all of the Julia Quinn source material in less than a week. Thank you for breaking the world record for e-book and audiobook consumption so that I could ramble at you about sexy ice cream and Regency tea parties. Love you, Mom.

—*Emily Timberlake*

THANK YOU TO THE LOVELY AND BRILLIANT EMILY TIMBERLAKE. YOU ARE a joy to work with and generous in every way possible. I am forever indebted to you for allowing me to text you at all hours of the day to brainstorm recipe ideas. I could not imagine working on this cookbook with anyone else. It is wonderful humans like you that remind me why I love what I do for a living.

I am endlessly grateful to Sarah Malarkey for allowing my voice and creativity to shine in the projects that we have brought to life together. Lydia Estrada, thank you for all that you do BTS to keep us on track. Thank you to Shonda Rhimes for creating television that an Asian-American woman like myself can watch and see herself in (Christina Yang forever). Thank you to the extraordinary Shondaland team for being the ultimate authorities in all things *Bridgerton*. I could not have created these recipes without your guidance and thoughtful feedback.

Lastly, thank you to Vanessa Cunto, Ali Clarke, Santos Loo, and Madhuri Sharma for your incredible insight and support while I cooked my way through the Regency era.

—*Susan Vu*

Index

Note: Page references in *italics* indicate photographs.

Published in the United States by RANDOM HOUSE WORLDS, an imprint of RANDOM HOUSE, a division of PENGUIN RANDOM HOUSE LLC, New York.
RandomHouseBooks.com

RANDOM HOUSE is a registered trademark, and RANDOM HOUSE WORLDS and colophon are trademarks of PENGUIN RANDOM HOUSE LLC.

Library of Congress Cataloging-in-Publication Data
Names: Timberlake, Emily, author. | Vu, Susan, author. Title: The Official Bridgerton Guide to Entertaining: How to Cook, Host, and Toast Like a Member of the Ton / Emily Timberlake, Susan Vu. Description: First edition. | New York : Penguin Random House, [2023]. | Includes index. Identifiers: LCCN 2023021511 (print) | LCCN 2023021512 (ebook) | ISBN 9780593796238 (board) | ISBN 9780593796245 (ebk) Subjects: LCSH: Dinners and dining. | Cooking. | Bridgerton (Television | LCGFT: Cookbooks.
Classification: LCC TX737 .T55 2023 (print) | LCC TX737 (ebook) | DDC 641.5/4—dc23/eng/20230508
LC record available at https://lccn.loc .gov/2023021511
LC ebook record available at https://lccn .loc.gov/2023021512

Hardcover ISBN 978-0-593-79623-8
Ebook ISBN 978-0-593-79624-5

Printed in the United States of America on acid-free paper

Unit photography courtesy NETFLIX/LIAM DANIEL

Hand-lettering on page 31 by SCHIN LOONG

Illustrations on pages 14, 40, 68, 98, and 132 by VEXELS

Editor: SARAH MALARKEY
Production editor: PATRICIA SHAW
Editorial assistant: LYDIA ESTRADA
Art director and designer: IAN DINGMAN
Photography by: LIZZIE MUNRO
Food stylist: BRETT REGOT
Food styling assistant: PAUL WANG
Prop stylist: ANDREA GRECO
Prop stylist assistants: TODD HENRY and ASHLEIGH SARBONE
Photo assistants: PARIS BENSON and TRISHA PICKELHAUPT
Production manager: JESSICA HEIM
Recipe developer: SUSAN VU
Copyeditor: ANDREA CHESMAN
Proofreaders: MARTHA SCHWARTZ and LORIE YOUNG
Indexer: ELIZABETH T. PARSON

1st Printing

First Edition